D1439842

Resource Pack
for
Assessment for Learning
in
Mathematics

Edited by Doug French

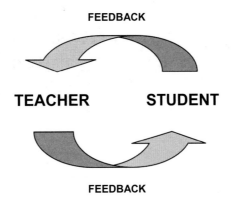

FEEDBACK

TEACHER   STUDENT

FEEDBACK

THE MATHEMATICAL ASSOCIATION
supporting mathematics in education

A1100823

Assessment for Learning

Research-based principles of assessment for learning to guide classroom practice

© Assessment Reform Group, 2002

Assessment for Learning is the process of seeking and interpreting evidence for use by learners and their teachers to decide where the learners are in their learning, where they need to go and how best to get there.

Inner ring

- is part of effective planning
- focuses on how students learn
- is central to classroom practice
- is a key professional skill
- is sensitive and constructive
- fosters motivation
- promotes understanding of goals and criteria
- helps learners know how to improve
- develops the capacity for self-assessment
- recognises all educational achievement

Assessment for learning should be part of effective planning of teaching and learning

A teacher's planning should provide opportunities for both learner and teacher to obtain and use information about progress towards learning goals. It also has to be flexible to respond to initial and emerging ideas and skills. Planning should include strategies to ensure that learners understand the goals they are pursuing and the criteria that will be applied in assessing their work. How learners will receive feedback, how they will take part in assessing their learning and how they will be helped to make further progress should also be planned.

Assessment for learning should focus on how students learn

The process of learning has to be in the minds of both learner and teacher when assessment is planned and when the evidence is interpreted. Learners should become as aware of the 'how' of their learning as they are of the 'what'.

Assessment for learning should be recognised as central to classroom practice

Much of what teachers and learners do in classrooms can be described as assessment. That is, tasks and questions prompt learners to demonstrate their knowledge, understanding and skills. What learners say and do is then observed and interpreted, and judgements are made about how learning can be improved. These assessment processes are an essential part of everyday classroom practice and involve both teachers and learners in reflection, dialogue and decision making.

Assessment for learning should be regarded as a key professional skill for teachers

Teachers require the professional knowledge and skills to: plan for assessment; observe learning; analyse and interpret evidence of learning; give feedback to learners and support learners in self-assessment. Teachers should be supported in developing these skills through initial and continuing professional development.

Assessment for learning should be sensitive and constructive because any assessment has an emotional impact

Teachers should be aware of the impact that comments, marks and grades can have on learners' confidence and enthusiasm and should be as constructive as possible in the feedback that they give. Comments that focus on the work rather than the person are more constructive for both learning and motivation.

Assessment should take account of the importance of learner motivation

Assessment that encourages learning fosters motivation by emphasising progress and achievement rather than failure. Comparison with others who have been more successful is unlikely to motivate learners. It can also lead to their withdrawing from the learning process in areas where they have been made to feel they are 'no good'. Motivation can be preserved and enhanced by assessment methods which protect the learner's autonomy, provide some choice and constructive feedback, and create opportunity for self-direction.

Assessment for learning should promote commitment to learning goals and a shared understanding of the criteria by which they are assessed

For effective learning to take place learners need to understand what it is they are trying to achieve - and want to achieve it. Understanding and commitment follows when learners have some part in deciding goals and identifying criteria for assessing progress. Communicating assessment criteria involves discussing them with learners using terms that they can understand, providing examples of how the criteria can be met in practice and engaging learners in peer- and self-assessment.

Learners should receive constructive guidance about how to improve

Learners need information and guidance in order to plan the next steps in their learning. Teachers should: pinpoint the learner's strengths and advise on how to develop them; be clear and constructive about any weaknesses and how they might be addressed; provide opportunities for learners to improve upon their work.

Assessment for learning develops learners' capacity for self-assessment so that they can become reflective and self-managing

Independent learners have the ability to seek out and gain new skills, new knowledge and new understandings. They are able to engage in self-reflection and to identify the next steps in their learning. Teachers should equip learners with the desire and the capacity to take charge of their learning through developing the skills of self-assessment.

Assessment for learning should recognise the full range of achievements of all learners

Assessment for learning should be used to enhance all learners' opportunities to learn in all areas of educational activity. It should enable all learners to achieve their best and to have their efforts recognised.

Resource Pack for Assessment for Learning in Mathematics

Preface

Assessment for learning, or formative assessment, is increasingly being recognised as a vital tool in the endeavour to improve the quality of learning in mathematics at all levels. It involves a number of key principles and simple procedures which should become part of the daily classroom practice of every teacher. It stands in stark contrast to the tests and examinations that characterise summative assessment, whose current dominance commonly detracts from building students' confidence and enjoyment of mathematics and gives them little help to improve their current knowledge and understanding.

In essence assessment for learning involves gathering frequent detailed evidence of students' current understanding in many different ways, in the light of which specific advice can be given about what they should do to improve. It involves actively engaging students in seeking to improve their own learning by being much more explicit about what they can do to help themselves rather than by just urging them to 'learn things properly' or 'try harder'.

This book provides a discussion of the key principles and procedures and relates these to a wide variety of classroom examples and resources which we hope teachers will find a valuable source of ideas that they can incorporate readily into their daily classroom practice. Many of the ideas involve small changes which do not require a lot of time or effort to prepare and are easy to put into practice. Introducing such small changes thoughtfully over a period of time can have a big impact on the quality of students' learning and on their attitudes towards mathematics.

The pack includes a CD-ROM with whiteboard masters and many other useful resources.

Acknowledgements

The book has been produced by the members of the 11 to 16 sub-committee of the Teaching Committee of the Mathematical Association and has been edited by Doug French. The members of the sub-committee who have contributed to the book are:

Robin Bevan	Sue Forrest	Mary Ledwick
Christine Brown	Doug French	Amanda Longstaff
Barbara Cullingworth	Jennie Golding	Sue Waring
Steve Edwards	Jenni Ingram	

The members of the sub-committee would particularly like to record their thanks to all the members of both Teaching Committee and Publications Committee and to the office staff at the Association's headquarters in Leicester for all their support and help as this book has been prepared for publication. We are also grateful to the Assessment Reform Group for permission to reproduce their Assessment for Learning poster.

Contents

Introduction

What is Assessment for Learning?   1

Why is Assessment for Learning important?   2

How does Assessment for Learning differ from other forms of assessment?   3

What factors underpin successful Assessment for Learning?   4

Lesson objectives   5

Asking questions and giving feedback   7

Monitoring progress during a lesson   17

Advice on improving   19

Written feedback   21

Self and peer assessment   24

Tasks and Tools to promote Assessment for Learning

Using mini-whiteboards   26

Using matching cards   27

Using posters   28

Students producing their own resources   29

Topic-based Classroom Resources

Reviewing and summarising   31

Number   43

Algebra   49

Geometry   59

Probability and statistics   66

Bibliography   73

Appendix

Three articles from *Equals* by Dylan Wiliam   75

University of Worcester
A1100822

Assessment for Learning in Mathematics

What is Assessment for Learning?

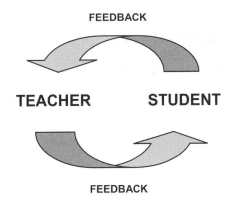

Assessment for Learning is the process of seeking and interpreting evidence for use by learners and their teachers to decide where the learners are in their learning, where they need to go and how best to get there.

Assessment Reform Group (2002)

Assessment for learning, or **formative assessment**, is any form of assessment where the main objective is to improve directly the quality of students' learning. An assessment activity becomes formative assessment when the evidence it provides is used to modify teaching and learning activities so that students have immediate ways of improving on their current understanding and performance. It contrasts with **summative assessment**, whose purpose is primarily to provide a judgement after the event about what learning has taken place.

Successful classroom teachers assess almost continuously: it becomes assessment for learning when the information is used to help students improve as difficulties arise and to guide planning for future work. Increasingly, there is evidence that assessment for learning becomes even more powerful when it is understood and accepted by students as something to which they can contribute and from which they can acquire detailed ways to improve and to be more successful.

The key message for every teacher in every lesson is:

- GATHER EVIDENCE.
- PROVIDE FEEDBACK.
- IMPROVE LEARNING.

Why is Assessment for Learning important?

There have been few initiatives in education with such a strong body of evidence to support a claim to raise standards.

Working inside the Black Box
Paul Black et al (2002)

Effective formative assessment is a key factor in motivating learning and raising pupils' standards of achievement.

Good Assessment Practice in Mathematics
Ofsted (2003)

Inside the Black Box, by Black and Wiliam (1998), provides substantial evidence from a wide range of research studies from many countries that improving formative assessment raises standards. Enhancing the way that assessment is used in the classroom to promote learning has been shown to have the effect, in England, of increasing achievement by the equivalent of between one and two GCSE grades per student on average and, moreover, the gain is often greatest for the lower achieving students.

ASSESSMENT FOR LEARNING ⇒ HIGHER STANDARDS

Successful assessment for learning improves the motivation and confidence of students and helps to build a cycle of ever improving success with learning. That is true in the both short term and the long term, as this approach to learning helps to build positive attitudes and valuable skills that are retained for lifelong learning. This is increasingly important in a society of rapid and continuing change.

Effective assessment practice in mathematics is associated with systematic arrangements for actively promoting, monitoring and recording pupils' progress. In such circumstances, assessment is used as a teaching tool as well as a means of judging attainment. At best teachers review pupils' progress closely as part of daily classroom practice, involving pupils in the assessment of their strengths and weaknesses and provide feedback on how to improve.

Good Assessment Practice in Mathematics
Ofsted (2003)

The message about feedback on how to improve is very clear:

BETTER FEEDBACK ⇒ BETTER LEARNING

2

How does Assessment for Learning differ from other forms of assessment?

*A clear distinction should be made between **assessment of learning** for the purposes of grading and reporting, which has its own well established procedures, and **assessment for learning** which calls for different priorities, new procedures and a new commitment.*

Assessment for learning: beyond the black box
Assessment Reform Group (1999)

Assessment designed primarily for the purposes of accountability or of certifying competence has an important role, but this assessment **of** learning, known as **summative assessment** is in itself of limited value in extending the individual student's knowledge and understanding. An end-of-unit test may be used simply to record evidence of a mark or level achieved by students at that point in time. Only when the assessment is considered in more detail, and the implications for teaching and learning followed into practice, does it become **formative assessment** which can benefit the students directly. Inappropriate summative assessment, in contrast, often lowers the self-esteem of students and discourages learning.

ASSESSMENT OF LEARNING (AOL) - SUMMATIVE ASSESSMENT

ASSESSMENT FOR LEARNING (AFL) - FORMATIVE ASSESSMENT

Summative assessment can be used in a formative way if the evidence from a test is used by the teacher, or by individual students, to analyse current strengths and weaknesses and thus to determine future teaching and learning strategies. When this occurs, whether immediately or at some time in the future, then that summative assessment is being used formatively. The same would be true on any scale, whether it be marking of a single homework or an end-of-key-stage test. However, assessment **for** learning, or formative assessment, is not just a matter of making better use of the data that arise from summative assessment. Marking which simply highlights errors is not sufficient to improve learning.

SUMMATIVE ASSESSMENT - SUMMARISES ATTAINMENT

FORMATIVE ASSESSMENT - IMPROVES LEARNING

The high-stakes nature of much present summative assessment unfortunately encourages teachers to focus on practising test-taking rather than on using assessment to support learning with understanding. We need to have confidence in the abundant evidence that investing time and effort in implementing good learning practices in our classrooms will result in students with better motivation and understanding, who will then, incidentally, also achieve more highly in summative assessments.

What factors underpin successful Assessment for Learning?

The research indicates that improving learning through assessment depends on five, deceptively simple, key factors:

- *the provision of effective feedback to pupils;*

- *the active involvement of pupils in their own learning;*

- *adjusting teaching to take account of the results of assessment;*

- *a recognition of the profound influence assessment has on the motivation and self-esteem of pupils, both of which are crucial influences on learning;*

- *the need for pupils to be able to assess themselves and understand how to improve.*

> *Assessment for learning: beyond the black box*
> Assessment Reform Group (1999)

Assessment for learning is in principle a simple idea which should be embedded in the repertoire of practices used constantly by every teacher. For the most part it is not something that is independent of the normal everyday talk and tasks of the classroom, but incorporating it should have a considerable influence on the nature of those activities. It does not necessarily involve substantial immediate change to current practice, because small changes can make a huge difference. For example, using mini-whiteboards with a class to get feedback as a lesson progresses or writing appropriate comments rather than giving marks or grades for some pieces of homework are small changes that can make a big difference.

SMALL CHANGES CAN MAKE A BIG DIFFERENCE.

Feedback is a key idea with assessment for learning: evidence of understanding needs to be obtained, interpreted and acted upon. This may mean that a little more time needs to be spent discussing a new idea before proceeding, because an unexpected misconception has arisen or a particular skill required for the next step has not been fully mastered. Lesson planning needs to be flexible, to allow for changes of direction and timing as students' responses to the material emerge and also for the effective use of 'wrong answers' as points for discussion.

It is important to recognise the profound influence that assessment has on students' motivation. Even for the most successful students, an over-emphasis on marks and grades focuses their attention on how to achieve better marks rather than on how to make better sense of the mathematical ideas. For many students, frequent low marks and critical comments are constant blows to their self-esteem and confidence. Assessment for learning does not focus on marks: it focuses on helping students to improve by identifying sources of difficulty as they arise and by reacting with suitably detailed advice.

Lesson Objectives

OBJECTIVES: IDEAS TO BE LEARNT, NOT JUST TASKS TO DO

If assessment for learning is to be successful, research shows that learners need to understand what they are trying to achieve. Sharing learning objectives with students ensures that they are aware of what they are learning and why. Objectives need to be expressed in a language that students understand, but there are many ways of sharing them with students:

- Objectives on the board throughout a lesson;

- Objectives shared orally;

- As a question which students are working towards being able to answer;

- As a surprise where students are made aware of that as the intention and are shown what they have achieved at an appropriate point.

Learning objectives need to be set in the context of past and future learning, and they should be **related to what is to be learnt, not to the task or activity** which has been designed to help achieve that end. For example, an objective like 'to able to calculate the third side of a right-angled triangle given two sides' makes clear what students are expected to be able to do successfully, whereas 'to complete Exercise 2B, questions 1 to 10' or 'to complete the worksheet on Pythagoras' theorem' only tells them what task they have to complete.

Good practice involves having appropriate, clear and precise learning objectives, and using them in every lesson to maintain a focus on what is being learned. It involves structuring lessons to provide opportunities to focus on each learning objective, and to review them at intervals, through approaches such as questioning, peer and self assessment, written and oral feedback. There needs to be flexibility according to the outcomes of these approaches and clarity about what the teacher expects students to do to be able to demonstrate achievement. However, it is very important to recognise that learning outcomes other than those planned can also be valuable! Opportunities to explore interesting ideas that arise unexpectedly should certainly be exploited as a natural part of any lesson.

KNOW WHERE YOU ARE GOING, BUT ADJUST YOUR TIMING
AND YOUR OBJECTIVES AS YOU PROCEED.

Commonly used stems for framing learning objectives include:

- To be able to define …
- To be able to calculate …
- To be able to construct …

- To understand …
- To be able to make connections between …
- To be able to explain …

A set of learning objectives for a sequence of lessons on Pythagoras' theorem:

- To be able to identify the hypotenuse of a right-angled triangle.

- To understand the relationship between the sides of a right-angled triangle.

- To be able to calculate the hypotenuse of a right-angled triangle given the other two sides.

- To be able to calculate the third side of a right-angled triangle given the other two sides.

- To understand how to check whether a calculated length is sensible in relation to the given sides.

- To know how to round lengths to a suitable degree of accuracy.

- To be able to draw a rough diagram from a word problem involving right-angled triangles.

- To be able to solve simple problems involving lengths where a right-angled triangle has to be identified such as finding the height of an isosceles triangle given the sides.

Some objectives refer to definitions or procedures which can be demonstrated readily and will provide a typical reference point to check whether a fact has been remembered or a skill mastered. Other objectives, such as those referring to understanding or making connections, are vaguer and longer term because they refer to aspects of learning which continue to develop over a long period even for seemingly elementary matters. An understanding of Pythagoras' theorem is something which develops and extends over many years and is not complete after a single sequence of lessons, however complete the mastery of the material of those particular lessons. There are always new insights to be acquired.

- Have students encountered more than one simple way of proving Pythagoras' theorem?

- Students may know about 3-4-5 triangles, but do they know of any more of these Pythagorean triples? Can they find any ways of doing this systematically? Is 3-4-5 the only Pythagorean triple consisting of three consecutive numbers?

- Have your A level students realised that the cosine rule is a generalisation of Pythagoras' theorem when the right angle is varied?

Asking Questions and Giving Feedback

How many centimetres in a metre?	100

- How do you respond to a student who says 1000?

- What do a centimetre and 10 centimetres and a metre look like?

- What other words remind you of 100? Century, centipede, cent and centurion are obvious suggestions.

Even simple questions like this offer the possibility of feedback – it is not just a matter of saying whether the response is right or wrong. Feedback should provide ways to help students get it right on another occasion. Encouraging them to think of links is often useful so that it is not just a matter of memorising an isolated fact. Oral feedback is immediate and context-specific and it can be adaptable, stimulating, versatile and motivating. It does not always require an immediate indication as to whether a response is correct or not. A further question is often a good tactic – and not just in following on from an incorrect answer.

Effective oral questioning and feedback takes time to develop, needs to be planned, and requires fostering within a supportive learning environment. It may be direct, by targeting individuals or groups, or indirect, as when others listen and reflect on what is being said. It takes a surprisingly short time to develop a supportive culture in a classroom and to establish that your own and students' errors are learning opportunities, but it requires perseverance and the creative use of questions and comments.

How many lines of symmetry has a square?	4

- 1, 2 and 4 are common answers; 3 is not unknown.

- Ask students to draw a square and mark the lines of symmetry or cut out a paper square and try folding it.

- Try turning the square through 45°: is it harder or easier to see the 4 lines of symmetry?

- Ask how many ways you can cut a square in half. This is an example of a 'rich' follow-up question where there is some ambiguity and where ideas involving rotational symmetry may arise.

- Why are the symmetries of a rectangle and a rhombus different?

It is important to allow sufficient 'wait time' when questioning. Students need time to think. There are many strategies which can help with this besides those associated with using mini-whiteboards which are discussed in a later section of the book:

- Make a conscious effort to pause before asking for responses – this encourages everybody to think, including those who tend to respond impulsively with inappropriate guesses. Explain why you are pausing.

- Establish a 'no hands up' rule so that you choose who responds after a suitable interval.

- Tell students to write down their response and then ask individuals what they have written. Requiring a written response ensures that a higher proportion of the class does think about the question.

- Ask students to brainstorm ideas in pairs or small groups before asking for responses.

Time for individual feedback is limited, and there is a danger that fast-paced question and answer sessions may be mistaken for fast-paced learning. Instant feedback often focuses on getting right answers and giving praise and encouragement rather than on developing students' understanding. There is room for both, of course, but feedback should seek to extend their understanding and to give them ways of thinking about their responses. This applies to the simplest questions, even those which seem to be a matter of recalling a fact or performing a simple calculation.

How many faces on a cuboid?	6	What is a cuboid? What shape are its faces? How do you know that there are 6? Top, bottom, front, back, left and right.
How many centimetres approximately in an inch?	2·5	What does an inch look like? And a centimetre? So how many roughly? Look at a ruler. How many in a foot?
How many thousands in one million?	1000	How many thousands in 5000? How many in 80000? How do you work it out? How do you write a million?
What is 5×7?	35	What is 2×7 and then 4×7? How about 10×7? How can these help you to work it out? What is 5×14 and 5×24?

Feedback often takes the form of further questions, as in these examples, because that can help students to think again and see that there are alternative ways of working things out or ways of relating questions to other more familiar ideas. Questions can take many different forms:

- What makes you say that?

- How can you be sure?

- Why do you think he/she said that?

- What else can you say about it?

- How do you write that?

- Can you suggest another question like this?

- Is there a **simpler** question that you **can** work out?

- Can you suggest an approximate answer?

- Is that a sensible answer?

It is not only the type of question that promotes understanding and gives valuable feedback, but the way in which questions and answers are used during a lesson. Askew and Lodge (2000) have classified classroom feedback at one of three levels, with the associated diagrams based on their work shown below.

Traditional classroom

Feedback is a one-way process (a gift), where the teacher acts as 'expert' giving information to others to help them improve.

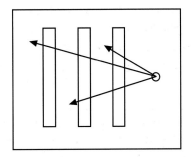

Enhanced classroom

Feedback is a two-way process (ping-pong), where the teacher enables others to gain new understandings, make sense of experiences and use open questions and shared insight to make connections.

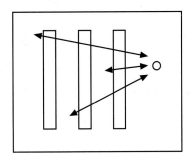

Expanded classroom

Feedback is a dialogue (loops), where classroom talk involves students commenting on other student's contributions with explicit discussion of 'how I am thinking'.

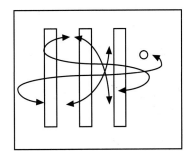

The type of questions asked influences the nature of the evidence that is obtained about students' skills and understanding. That in turn influences the nature of the feedback that the teacher can give to the student. Some questions will be designed to check whether students can remember facts or carry out simple skills, but others should be used to check on understanding, to use familiar ideas in different contexts and to encourage higher-order thinking skills.

Questions and tasks need to be planned to encourage higher level thinking as well as a way of checking on simple facts and skills. Time has to be spent in framing questions that are worth asking, so students realise that learning depends less on their capacity to spot the right answer and more on their readiness to think for themselves and discuss their own understanding.

Dylan Wiliam (1999), in an excellent article in *Equals* (see page 75), speaks of **rich questions** as ones that give particularly useful evidence about students' thinking in that they may reveal misconceptions. This idea might be extended by saying:

> RICH QUESTIONS AND TASKS ⇒ RICH EVIDENCE

Such questions do not need to be questions about hard topics, but they will have a degree of ambiguity or openness or the potential to reveal misconceptions. They may well not be the sort of questions deemed appropriate for a conventional examination paper, for they questions are designed for a summative purpose. However, students' responses will provide useful evidence about their thinking and their misconceptions, together with opportunities to follow them up through individual and class discussion.

Here are some examples of short, but potentially rich, questions with some comments on the sort of misconceptions that can be revealed and how they might be followed up:

- Divide 321 by 3.

The common error here is to leave out the zero to give an answer of 17. Discussion should focus on what a sensible answer might be: what will it be roughly? What is 300 divided by 3?

- Calculate $2.5 \times 3.7 \times 4$.

It is all too easy blindly to try calculating 2.5×3.7 first without realising that $2.5 \times 4 = 10$ is the obvious first step. Students need to be encouraged to pause and think before proceeding with any calculation. It may mean that they have to do less work in the long run - an attractive possibility!

- Which is greater: 0.55 or 0.6?

0.55 is a common wrong response, because students with a poor understanding of decimals ignore the decimal point and say that 55 is greater than 6. A number line or money can provide helpful concrete representations, although with money some weak students may think that £0.6 is 6p.

- Give a number between 0.25 and 0.3

A response like 0.17 tells you that understanding of decimals is not secure!

- Can you simplify $3a + 2b$?

Typically this will lead some students to suggest 6ab as an answer. It is important to help them to see that such an answer is not sensible by seeing what happens when some numbers are substituted. For example with $a = 5$ and $b = 4$, $3a + 2b = 23$, but $6ab = 120$, so something must be wrong!

- What is the value of $5d^2$ when $d = 2$?

Debate which answer is correct – 20 or 100 – and talk about conventions in interpreting algebraic language. Finding the area of the cross below, where d is the edge of a square, reinforces the meaning of the algebraic expression.

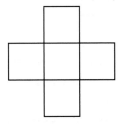

- If n is an integer, is $3n - 1$ always an odd number?

The presence of two odd numbers may make this look odd, but multiples of 3 can be either odd or even. A spreadsheet provides a nice illustration of this.

n	$3n$ -1
1	2
2	5
3	8
4	11
5	14

- All squares are rectangles. True or false?

Squares are often not seen as a special case of a rectangle. Discussion about definitions is valuable here: what is a rectangle? Does a square fit the same definition? Could a square be described as a rectangle with equal sides?

- Find the other angles if one angle of an isosceles triangle is 80°.

There is an element of ambiguity here because the 80° angle may be one of the pair of equal angles or it may be the vertical angle. Allowing students to spot this for themselves rather than telling them directly that there are two possibilities gives them more opportunity to think for themselves.

- Is it true with a set of data that about half the values will be above average?

This is true if the average is the median, but is not usually the case with the mean unless the distribution is symmetrical. Understanding the distinction between averages and the information they give needs careful discussion which goes beyond learning how to calculate them.

- Find a point on the line $y = 3x - 5$.

An open ended question, but it checks whether the idea of the equation has been understood.

- Give an equation of a straight line through the point $(2, 3)$.

This is a very useful starting point for checking and developing understanding of equations and the significance of gradient.

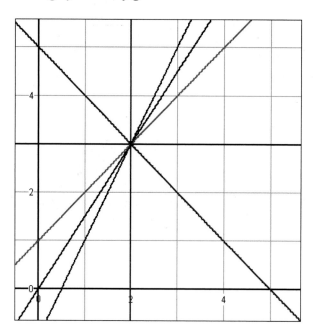

- Find the area of a rectangle with a perimeter of 20cm.

There are, of course, many possible answers! It is often useful to draw diagrams to illustrate the variety of shapes with a common perimeter. Frequent discussion involving concrete examples helps to break down the confusion that exists between area and perimeter. The question can be reversed by giving the area and asking for possible perimeters.

- Give two different fractions whose sum is ½.

This provides an alternative to the usual routine exercises on adding fractions. It can reveal misunderstandings and has the virtue of allowing weaker students to suggest simple examples whilst abler students can be more ambitious.

- Find a fraction that lies between ½ and ⅓.

This open ended question is likely to give rise to a variety of answers which will give valuable evidence about students' thinking and open up many possibilities for discussion and feedback. The table below shows some possible responses:

$\frac{2}{5}$	$\frac{1}{2} = 0.5$ and $\frac{1}{3} = 0.333...$ $0.4 = \frac{2}{5}$ is between them.
$\frac{2}{5}$	$\frac{1}{2.5}$ is between $\frac{1}{2}$ and $\frac{1}{3}$. $\frac{1}{2.5} = \frac{2}{5}$
$\frac{49}{100}$	Just less than a half, but nowhere near to $\frac{1}{3}$, which is about $\frac{33}{100}$.
$\frac{9}{20}$	0.45 is between $\frac{1}{2} = 0.5$ and $\frac{1}{3} = 0.333...$
$\frac{7}{20}$	0.35 is just a bit more than $\frac{1}{3} = 0.333...$.
$\frac{5}{12}$	$\frac{1}{2} = \frac{6}{12}$ and $\frac{1}{3} = \frac{4}{12}$. $\frac{5}{12}$ is between.
$\frac{5}{12}$	$\frac{1}{2} + \frac{1}{3} = \frac{5}{6}$. Dividing by 2 gives $\frac{5}{12}$, which is the mean.

Further possibilities:

between $\frac{1}{2}$ and $\frac{2}{3}$, less than $\frac{1}{10}$, less than $\frac{1}{100}$, between $\frac{2}{5}$ and $\frac{3}{7}$.

Something to consider:

Why is $\frac{a+b}{c+d}$ always between $\frac{a}{c}$ and $\frac{b}{d}$ where a, b, c and d are positive integers?

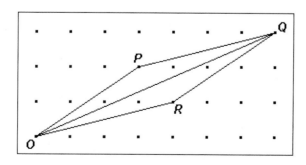

Compare the gradients of *OP*, *OR* and *OQ* represented in the diagram by the three fractions: $\frac{2}{3}$, $\frac{1}{4}$ and $\frac{3}{7} = \frac{2+1}{3+4}$.

Short sets of questions, like those that follow, can be used at one of several different points during a lesson – at the beginning to check on prior knowledge, during the lesson to check on understanding at that point or at the end as a final check up on the ideas of a lesson. The format of the questions can be varied to provide:

- the basis for a whole class discussion;

- for discussion in small groups either with reporting back to the whole class or with the drawing up of a poster or an OHP slide;

- a sequence of questions using mini-whiteboards;

- for individual students to produce written responses which are assessed by the teacher or by one of their peers.

Some questions about Pythagoras' theorem

Objectives:

- to be able to calculate the third side given two sides of a right-angled triangle;

- to understand how to check whether a calculated length is sensible in relation to the given sides.

Some questions:

The third sides of the triangles have lengths of $\sqrt{3} \approx 1.7$ and $\sqrt{5} \approx 2.2$.

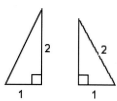

- Which length goes with which triangle?

- Explain how you know.

- How were the two lengths calculated?

The emphasis in obtaining feedback here is not on whether the students can do the calculations to get correct answers, but on asking them to explain how given answers have been obtained and to use the properties of the triangles to decide which answers are sensible for each. This is done in the context of two examples which are commonly confused and is therefore potentially useful in highlighting which students are continuing to have difficulties in deciding between $2^2 + 1^2$ and $2^2 - 1^2$ as the square of the unknown side. It also emphasises the importance of checking that answers are sensible and provides an opportunity to discuss how to do this.

Some questions about isosceles triangles

Objectives:

- to understand the relationship between the angles of an isosceles triangle;

- to be able to spot isosceles triangles in diagrams, particularly those involving circles;

- to be able to present a simple chain of reasoning in calculating angles.

Some questions:

In the diagram, C is the centre of the semi-circle. The missing angles are 25°, 130°, 50°, 65° and 65°.

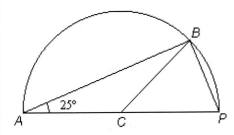

- Put the missing angles in the right positions.

- Explain how you know.

- What can you say about $\angle ABP$?

- What are the angles if $\angle PAB = 35°$? What is $\angle ABP$?

- What are the angles if $\angle PAB = x°$? What is $\angle ABP$?

- What is always true about $\angle ABP$?

The emphasis in the first part is to see that the students can spot the two isosceles triangles and then deduce the positions of the given angles. Providing the values of the angles makes this a task which is self-checking. The second part requires them to express their reasoning coherently and the third part hints at the angle in a semi-circle property.

The next set of three questions requires them to calculate another set of angles to check that the deduction procedure is understood and then to generalise by expressing the angles in terms of the variable x, leading them on to prove that the angle in a semi-circle is a right angle.

For some students, only the questions based on numerical values will be appropriate; for others the task could be extended by, for example, providing a diagram that will lead to a proof that the angle at the centre is double the angle at the centre standing on the same arc.

Some questions about a distance time graph

Objectives:

- to understand the relationship between distance and time on a graph and to be able to describe in detail the journey it portrays;

- to appreciate the significance of gradient in representing velocity (speed and direction);

- to be able to calculate the velocity given by the gradient of a line.

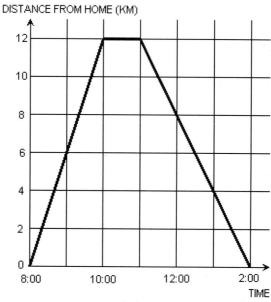

- Describe in as much detail as possible the journey represented by this graph.

- Another person sets out from the same place at 10:00am walking at 6km/h. At what time and where will the two people pass each other?

The first part is to check that the students can use all the information given by the graph, including velocities to describe the journey. The second question checks their ability to create a graph of their own where velocity is given and to see the significance of the intersection of two lines.

An alternative would be to give the story, as below, and ask the students to produce a graph.

A person sets out from home at 8:00am and walks at 6km/h for two hours and then rests for an hour before returning more slowly at 4km/h. How far did the person walk and at what time did they arrive home?

Monitoring Progress during a Lesson

> HOW DO YOU KNOW, AS A LESSON PROCEEDS, THE EXTENT TO WHICH EACH STUDENT IS MAKING SENSE OF WHAT THEY ARE BEING ASKED TO DO?
>
> HOW DO YOU OBTAIN FEEDBACK FROM EVERY STUDENT DURING EACH LESSON?
>
> HOW DO YOU GIVE STUDENTS SPECIFIC ADVICE ABOUT PARTICULAR TOPICS TO HELP IMPROVE THEIR UNDERSTANDING AND SKILLS?

Obtaining frequent feedback from **all** students as a lesson proceeds, and responding to the evidence it gives, is an essential component of a good mathematics lesson. Questions to individuals may provide information about the understanding of a few students, but you also need simple ways to monitor the progress of everybody during a lesson, as a basis for proceeding. It is all too easy to assume that **all** is well when the minority of students who reply give appropriate responses with no significant errors.

Here are some simple ways of monitoring progress in the course of a lesson:

*   Ask students to write down their responses to oral questions. Then ask several individuals what they have written and put differing answers on the board. If they all agree, ask for any different answers. If several answers are given, get a show of hands for each answer, the result of which provides scope for further discussion.

*   Having set a routine exercise for a class, stop them when they should all have completed the first one or two questions and check, as with oral questions above. Do the same when answers to the rest of the exercise are discussed.

*   When they are working on a routine task, move round the room rapidly at an early stage and check that everybody has the first answer or two correct.

*   Give everybody a small piece of paper and ask them to write the answer to a key question without writing their name on the paper. Collect the papers, put them in random order and, as they watch, sort them into piles according to the answers given. This tells you everybody's response anonymously, whereas other ways of responding are much more public. You can cheat a bit so that the one isolated serious error has some apparent companions!

*   Whiteboards or digit cards can be used in a wide variety of ways, not just at the start of a lesson, but at intervals throughout a lesson, particularly as a check that new ideas are making sense.

*   Ask ambiguous or awkward questions – rich questions – so that students have to think, rather than just apply a rule blindly.

*   Ask pairs of students to find two or more different solutions to a problem such as drawing a rectangle with an area of 24cm^2.

- Let them have sufficient time to think when you ask an oral question. Pausing and waiting while for them to think is likely to lead to more thoughtful responses.

- Ask them to think silently first, and then to exchange and discuss answers in pairs or small groups to ensure that everyone becomes involved, before inviting responses for the class to consider.

- Traffic lights, thumbs up and smiley faces (from Wiliam in *Equals* on page 85) all provide ways of getting some feel for whether students are confident about a new idea or procedure, or about the answer to a question before telling them the correct response. However, it is very important to be aware that boys tend to be over optimistic and girls tend to under-estimate their capabilities.

- Any of theses techniques could be used either before or after an activity or task to assess progress.

	Green - I have no problems with this. Amber - I am not sure. Red - I have no idea at all.
	Thumbs up - fine. Thumbs down - I need some more help. Alternatively, use fingers as a 5 point measure from 5 for fine to 1 for no idea.
☺ ☺ ☹	Easy to understand. Not sure. It does not make sense.

Advice on Improving

> REMEMBERING KEY FACTS IS EASIER WHEN YOU UNDERSTAND.
>
> REMEMBERING IS HELPED BY MAKING LINKS TO OTHER IDEAS.
>
> YOU NEED WAYS OF WORKING OUT WHAT YOU MIGHT FORGET.

Generalised comments about working harder or trying harder, learning your tables or reading through your notes are not usually helpful. Students need specific guidance which is related to specific topics about what they can do to improve. Successful learning involves encouraging students to think and understand rather than merely remember. It is easier to remember what you understand - indeed it may well be that there is less to remember when you understand.

At a simple level, this can be applied to remembering the meanings of words by asking students to suggest related words which provide links, or by highlighting sources of confusion:

- octagon – a polygon with eight sides: compare octopus, octave, October (!);

- bilateral – two sided: compare bicycle and equilateral;

- transformation and translation – similar words, but distinct meanings;

- similar – a word with a precise mathematical meaning compared to the more general everyday meaning.

Applying this principle to multiplication tables consider the product 7×8 which features in *How Children Fail* by John Holt (1958) and is quoted in the *Mental Methods in Mathematics* by the Mathematical Association (1992). It is clearly vitally important at some stage that students can instantly recall the fact that $7 \times 8 = 56$, but it is more likely to be remembered if it is seen as something that is part of a rich network of interrelated ideas and procedures.

$$\boxed{7 \times 8} \qquad 7 \times 7 + 7 = 49 + 7 = 56$$
$$10 \times 7 - 14 \qquad = 70 - 14 = 56$$
$$2 \times 7 = 14 \;,\; 2 \times 14 = 28 \;;\; 2 \times 28 = 56$$
$$(\text{'double, double, double'})$$
$$5 \times 8 = 40 \qquad 2 \times 8 = 16 \qquad 40 + 16 = 56$$
$$\text{CALCULATE:} \quad 70 \times 8 \;,\; 7 \times 80 \;,\; 700 \times 80$$
$$0.7 \times 8 \;,\; 7 \times 0.8 \;,\; 0.7 \times 0.8$$
$$7 \times £0.80 \;,\; 70 \times £0.08$$

19

Advice about how to memorise such facts usually suggests rehearsing them constantly in a variety of ways, both publicly and privately. This may have some value, but giving students the security of being able to work out readily what they may forget is infinitely more valuable. Discussing alternative ways of calculating 7×8 both promotes understanding and develops more general skills. Highlighting multiplication facts that students have difficulty remembering and encouraging them to think of various ways of working them out and of applying them to other situations may be a better strategy than merely rehearsing the facts.

Practice does not always make perfect – being able to work things out from first principles is a valuable strategy when something has been forgotten. Being able to make links to related facts is very useful. For example, a student forgets the formula for the area of a parallelogram. Encourage them to make the link either to a rectangle – parallelogram has the same area as a rectangle on the same base, or to a triangle – parallelogram is made up of two congruent triangles.

Confidence is boosted if students have ways of seeing for themselves that their answers are correct. In this respect tasks which are self-checking are particularly valuable: for instance, those involving matching cards or those where a graph plotter tells you that you have found the straight line or curve that you want, because it passes through the right points.

Some things can be checked by doing them in a different way. With algebraic expressions, substituting numbers is helpful as a check, both with simplification tasks as well as, more obviously, when solving equations. Students should be constantly encouraged to ask themselves the all-important questions below as part of building their confidence in their ability to make sense of things and their willingness to keep trying with a problem until it does give a sensible answer.

> IS IT A SENSIBLE ANSWER?
>
> WHAT SHOULD IT BE ROUGHLY?
>
> HOW CAN I CHECK IT?

Written Feedback

- *A large proportion of written comments related to aspects other than the stated learning objectives of the task.*

- *Pupils recalled about one third of the written comments accurately.*

- *Pupils recalled proportionately more of the 'constructive' feedback and more of the feedback relating to learning objectives.*

- *The proportion of feedback which is constructive and related to objectives is greater in oral feedback than written.*

- *As more lengthy oral feedback is given, less of the earlier comments are retained.*

- *Individual verbal feedback, as opposed to whole-class feedback, improves the recollection of advice given.*

Marking and Feedback Michael Ronayne (1999)

Michael Ronayne's comments give food for thought about the nature and effectiveness of written feedback to students. It is the nature, rather than the quantity, of written feedback that is critical. Written comments need to be specific and detailed. Remarks like 'good' and 'try harder' do not provide students with ways of improving - and even 'good' students need to improve!

Comments on any piece of work should certainly include an element of praise, but they should also give some indication of how students can improve on their present level of understanding by referring to errors and other ways in which the quality of the work can be clarified or extended. Able students who get everything right should be constantly challenged by questions which will make them think round things further. Students should be praised with remarks directed at specific aspects of a task:

'I like your comment about the area of a parallelogram being twice the area of a triangle.'

'Good idea to check your answer like that.'

'Can you see what would happen if the triangle was not isosceles?'

Likewise when something is wrong, make specific suggestions:

'Check your solution to each equation to see if you are correct.'

'Look carefully to see how many more lines of symmetry there are - try turning the page round or cutting out a paper shape and folding.'

'Try to write several good short sentences to describe what you have noticed rather than just the key words.'

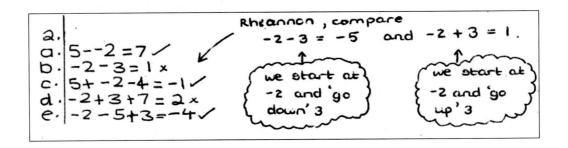

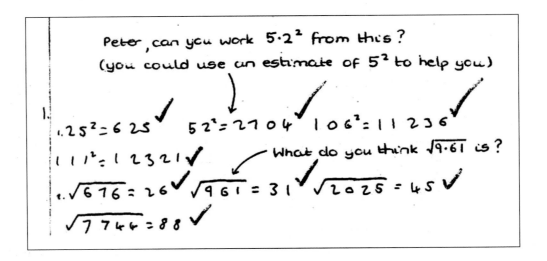

Comments should identify what has been done well, what needs improving and how that can be done. Where set questions have all been done correctly comments can challenge the student to think further. The teacher obviously requires a clear understanding of subject progression and the ability to recognise students' misconceptions and difficulties. Detailed marking of every aspect of every piece of written work is clearly unrealistic. Written tasks should be planned so that detailed marking is done when it is likely to be most productive.

Opportunities for students to follow up comments should be planned as part of the overall learning process: to be effective, feedback should cause thinking to take place. Seeking help is an essential part of their learning and leads to useful discussion about ways of learning. It is important that the whole process promotes, rather than damages, students' self-esteem and confidence: this will be enhanced if students feel that comments are detailed and useful.

Despite the overwhelming evidence, noted by Wiliam (1999) in *Equals* (see page 79), that the giving of marks or grades has a negative effect in that students ignore comments when marks are also given, many of us still persist with precisely that on a regular basis! A mark or grade does not tell students how to improve their work. There is no need to give a mark or grade for every piece of work, although it may be useful occasionally to give an indication of performance relative to a particular goal.

Students are certainly being prepared to take tests and examinations. However, it is not necessary or desirable that they are prepared either by constantly practising standard questions or by having every piece of work they do awarded a mark, as though it was yet another test. Frequent reference to marks, National Curriculum levels or predicted examination grades is very demoralising if they do not see how they can improve. It induces much stress even amongst those who may be highly successful. The important thing is to provide feedback which boosts confidence and shows students in simple terms the steps they can take to improve.

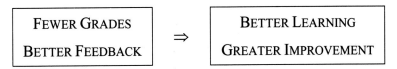

High quality feedback is expensive in terms of time and effort, of course. A single teacher has responsibility for five or more classes with thirty or more students in each. Weekly written feedback of good quality is not physically possible on this scale. Therefore there should be explicit expectations that detailed written feedback will be given periodically and selectively. These expectations should be incorporated into departmental and, preferably, school policy, so that there is a shared understanding between senior management, teachers, students and parents.

Broadening the range of approaches to marking requires planning the assessment strategy before a task begins **and** informing the students. Too often marking either focuses on students' answers only – devaluing the vital importance of method – or else it emphasises features of the work that students had not been alerted to beforehand.

Possible approaches are illustrated by the following examples:

For homework, please do questions 1 to 10. Use the first seven questions to build your confidence. I will only mark the last three and I will look carefully at the details of your method.

Complete the graph question and then use a coloured pen to highlight ten features that you would check if you were marking it!

Self and Peer Assessment

Self-assessment is an essential part of effective learning: as students begin to develop an overview of where they are going and why, it becomes possible for them to manage and control it for themselves, something which is increasingly important in the context of lifelong learning.

Peer-assessment turns out to be an important complement to self-assessment: students may accept from one another criticisms they might not take seriously from a teacher, and interchange will be in a language that students themselves use. They internalise lessons learned during peer-assessment, applying them to their own work, and, in a supportive climate, disagreement about assessment is thoroughly and openly discussed until agreement is reached.

Assessment of this kind is only possible if students are clear about the objectives against which they are assessing pieces of work and if they recognise what constitutes a good piece of work. Thus it is important that the teacher provides them with models of good mathematical writing – solutions to problems or proofs which have a suitable level of clearly written explanation and correct use of mathematical symbols and vocabulary.

Teachers have an important role in modelling appropriate mathematical behaviour by producing clear solutions to problems and well-argued proofs which communicate the ideas clearly, succinctly and correctly. Students need to see plenty of examples of good mathematical writing, not just the solutions that are written out in the course of a lesson, but also examples of complete pieces of work that can be examined and discussed to highlight their good features. Looking at poor work and defective solutions can be beneficial as well in pointing to ways of improving. So here are some things to incorporate into lessons from time to time.

- Show students good responses and explain why they are good by annotating them to highlight key features.

- Ask students to highlight aspects of model solutions to explain why they are good.

- Show students poor responses and explain why they do not meet relevant criteria by highlighting particular shortcomings.

- Show students poor responses and ask them to explain why they do not meet relevant criteria.

Obviously, the criteria for evaluating any learning task must be made transparent to students to enable them to have a clear overview both of the objectives of their work and of what it means to complete it successfully. They need to be taught explicitly the habits and skills of collaboration, both because these are of intrinsic value and because peer-assessment can help develop the objectivity required for effective self-assessment. Student-led plenaries can build on shared learning outcomes to develop confidence and ownership.

These skills do not always come easily. It takes time and effort to develop them, but it will happen much more easily if there is a whole school policy to develop peer-assessment. Summative assessments can also be used formatively, with peer marking of test papers often being helpful. This is particularly useful if students are required first to formulate a mark scheme, or even to generate and then answer their own questions. Teachers can then use their time for discussion of the questions that give particular difficulty, with peer-tutoring tackling minority problems. There is no need to feel guilty about the moderate use of peer-tutoring: every teacher knows the greater depth of understanding required, and fostered, by having to explain ideas.

Here are some ways of introducing an element-of peer assessment.

- Compare work of peers against the learning objectives for the task and indicate how it could be improved.

- Compare work with a model solution and identify ways in which it could be improved or extended.

- Mark against a specific National Curriculum level or GCSE grade criteria.

- Devise a mark scheme for a task to identify the key points that should be taken into account.

- Construct tasks to check on the understanding of particular ideas.

All these considerations apply equally to self-assessment, but in addition traffic lights can be used by students to indicate levels of understanding by applying them to lists of learning objectives at the end of work on a topic. Smiley faces, 'thumbs up' or just putting 'question marks' in the margin beside items about which they are unsure can be used in the same way.

Some classes respond well to the use of 'learning diaries', where they focus regularly on what they have learned this week, what has caused them difficulty and what they need to focus on in the coming week. This is the way to encourage independent learning!

MODELLING: WHAT DOES A GOOD PIECE OF WORK LOOK LIKE?

MARKING: HOW CAN A PIECE OF WRITTEN WORK BE IMPROVED?

Tasks and Tools to promote Assessment for Learning

Using Mini-whiteboards

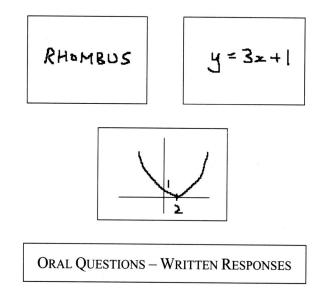

ORAL QUESTIONS – WRITTEN RESPONSES

Mini-whiteboards are only one medium for obtaining individual feedback, but they are powerful and simple. The essential idea with a whiteboard is that questions are asked orally, although they may be backed up by a written form or a diagram or graph, and that the questions require a written response – text, symbols or diagram – usually without any working being displayed. They have a number of particular advantages.

- Every student is involved.

- The teacher controls the pace when the boards are being used.

- Responses are not too public.

- Instant feedback is obtained from **all** students.

- Instant feedback can be given to students.

- It is possible to check that a key idea or procedure is clear before moving on.

It is a good idea to establish a routine when using boards so that all students have sufficient time to think and slower students do not feel undue pressure from those who want to respond quickly.

QUESTION → PAUSE, THINK AND WRITE → SHOW ME

Since students are often inclined to doodle inappropriately on their boards it is often worth asking everybody to reverse their boards ostensibly to show those behind them what they have written. Some teachers find that it is a useful idea at the start of a whiteboard session to give them a few minutes to draw a funny picture so that they 'let off steam' before settling down to the serious business of the lesson.

Individual whiteboards are available commercially or can be home-produced either by placing a sheet of A4 card in a transparent file sleeve or by laminating pieces of A4 card. A dry wipe pen and some form of eraser is required to go with each board. Boards created with card may be plain or spotty or they may display a pair of axes or a grid or diagram of some kind. A variety of examples of their use are given in this pack and various blank grids are provided on the accompanying CD-ROM. Alternatives such as digit cards and pairs of matching cards, discussed in the next section, can be used in a similar way to whiteboards.

Using Matching Cards

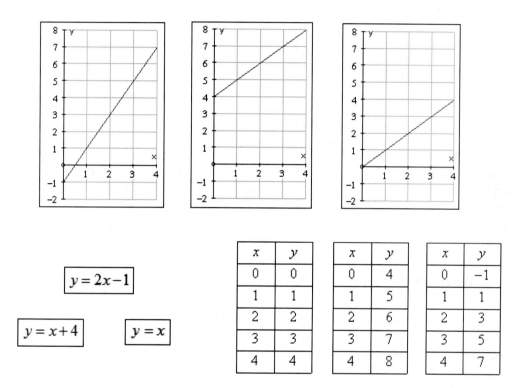

Tasks involving matching cards are very motivating and offer a valuable context which provides evidence of understanding and opportunities to offer students advice. Some of the particular advantages are as follows.

- High level of student engagement.

- Students are willing to discuss things in pairs and small groups.

- Responses are not too public and can be changed readily.

- Tasks provide evidence of misconceptions.

- Many opportunities to discuss difficulties with individuals and small groups.

- Strong motivation to persist until a problem is solved.

- Tasks are largely self-checking.

When a set of cards has been matched it can often be useful for students to record them either in their exercise books or on a poster, so that there is evidence of work done and the material is available for future reference in a suitable and correct form.

Items for cards can be created systematically on a grid and then the contents of the cards can be arranged randomly before printing them out. Students can then cut out the cards themselves. Cards do not always have to be produced in a printed format - they can often be hand written and photocopied as a way of producing a classroom task simply and rapidly.

Using Posters

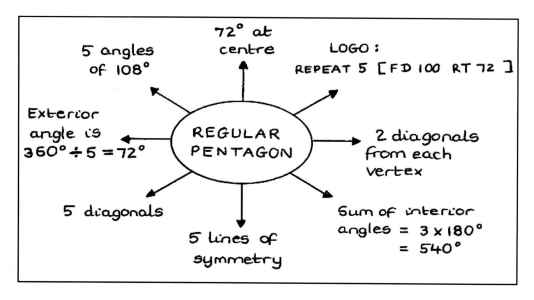

Asking groups of students to produce a poster to summarise the key ideas of a lesson or topic or to show how to solve a particular type of problem is a valuable task. It provides an excellent way of checking on understanding and identifying misconceptions and has the same sort of advantages as matching card tasks in providing both motivation to persist and plenty of feedback to the teacher on students' understanding of ideas.

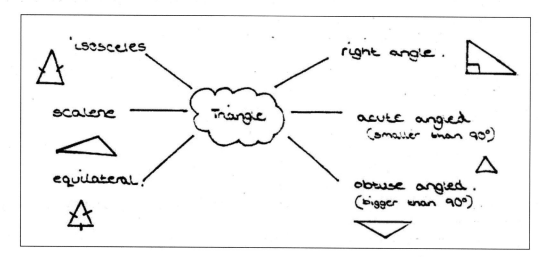

Students producing their own resources

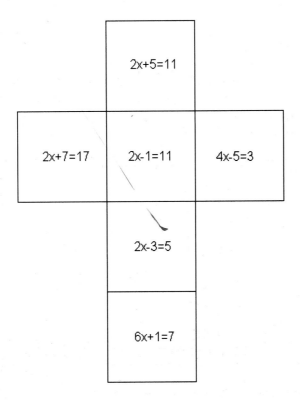

Create an equation dice.

The idea of students producing their own resources can be extended in a wide variety of ways. A student asked to solve twenty two-step linear equations will only think once, and will then repeat the 'recipe'. A student who is asked to produce five equations to be used as snakes and ladders cards, such as $2x + 5 = 11$ to move the bearer three squares, or equations to place on the six faces of a cube to make a dice as shown above, has to understand in depth what an equation is, in order to formulate one with an appropriate small integer solution. In addition, this can provide an incentive to work with negative numbers.

There is no comparison between the demands of the two tasks, and very often the teacher will see real comprehension dawn for the first time as the student works out how to formulate a 'clue'. As an assessment task, the latter demonstrates clearly whether the student understands how an equation works. If three or four such students then pool their cards and use them to play a game, peer assessment will be unrelenting until the mechanics of solution are also mastered. Teacher effort can then be used to listen and to intervene appropriately.

The same principle applies to writing – and answering – a small number of questions for homework with a selection being used in class next day. Writing dominoes or loop or snap cards uses the same principle. This technique for practising and assessing skills and understanding shows much more than whether students really understand an idea or procedure. It also differentiates in terms of outcome: students who feel very secure are much more adventurous with the numbers or the details of techniques that they use. This gives the teacher much richer evidence than typical text book exercises.

Making a set of dominoes provides another format, similar to that of matching cards, for each pair of students to make up questions and their answers. The topic and level of difficulty can be varied according to the students involved and there will be an element of differentiation by outcome. Swapping sets between pairs of students enables them to check what has been done and in so doing gives them a second opportunity to rehearse their skills and a further chance for the teacher to identify individual difficulties and discuss them. The diagram shows an example using percentages with money.

£0.80	12% of £50

£6	20% of £80

£16	25% of £30

£7.50	10% of £24

£2.40	75% of £18

£13.50	5% of £32

£1.60	20% of £12.50

£2.50	2% of £40

Make your own set of dominoes.

Topic-based Classroom Resources: Reviewing and Summarising

Starter activities are often designed to check on key ideas required for a lesson or to review a broader range of facts and skills. They can provide useful evidence as to whether individual students have remembered relevant facts and mastered particular skills and procedures, but it is also essential to probe deeper understanding and to extend thinking. This process of reviewing should not be confined to the start of a lesson, but should be something which features frequently at different points in a lesson – as a lesson proceeds to check on key points and at the end to review what has been done.

Short questions with a mini-whiteboard

At the simplest level, questions will be designed to check on simple facts and skills and any errors and misconceptions can be followed up. Mini-whiteboards are ideal for this purpose: the teacher asks a question, students write answers and then the teacher says 'show me', so that they reveal their boards simultaneously. Here are some examples of simple questions.

Lines of symmetry on a square?	4	Days in a leap year?	366
Metres in ¼ kilometre?	250	Vertices on a triangular prism?	6
3×29	87	Quadrilateral with two pairs of adjacent sides equal.	KITE
Kilogrammes in 3.5 tonnes?	3500	The mean of 5, 7 and 12.	8
What is 2^3 ?	8	Third angle of a triangle with angles of 50° and 70°?	60°
Evaluate $2a + 3b$ when $a = 5$ and $b = 4$.	22	Evaluate $2a^2$ when $a = 5$.	50

Questions can require a diagram as the response.

Draw two parallel lines and show me a pair of alternate angles.	
Draw an angle of approximately 120°.	
Draw a letter with 2 lines of symmetry.	
Draw me a trapezium.	
Draw a rectangle and shade in $\frac{2}{3}$ of it.	
Draw a line segment and sketch its perpendicular bisector.	
Sketch the graph of $y = \frac{1}{x}$.	

Using spider diagrams and mind maps

Ask students to work in pairs or small groups so that they can swap ideas. Ideas can then be presented as a poster, an overhead projector transparency or a PowerPoint slide. Students come to understand a variety of ideas – they are often more receptive to the ideas of their peers than those of their teachers. Besides providing an opportunity to share ideas, this type of activity is a rich source of assessment evidence as it reveals misconceptions and provides opportunities for the teacher to extend students' understanding. However, it can be difficult to express the steps of mental calculations in a correct mathematical form.

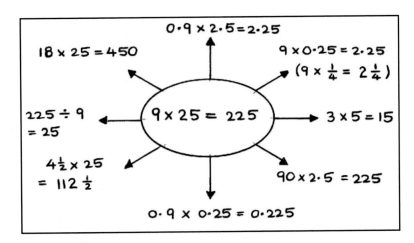

What else can you work out from $9 \times 25 = 225$?

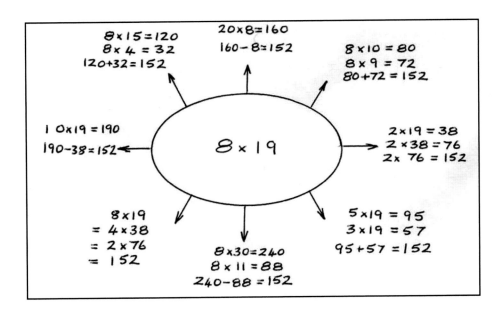

How many ways can you work out 8×19?

- Which method is best? Why?
- Which do you like? Why?
- Which is the neatest? Why?

- Which would you usually use? Why?
- Which wouldn't you use? Why?
- Which are confusing? Why?

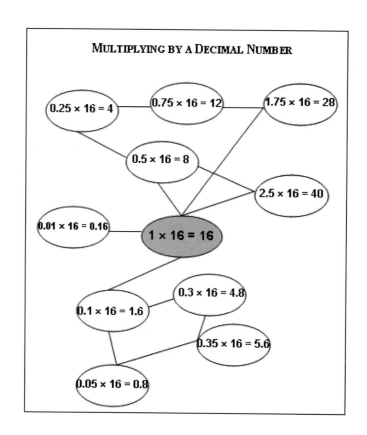

What can you work out from $1 \times 16 = 16$?

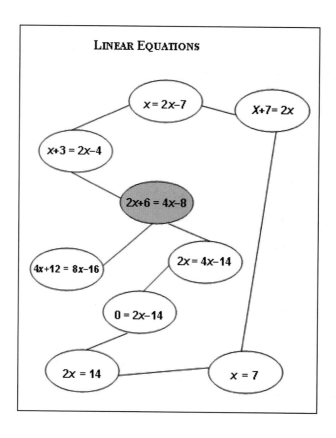

What other equations are equivalent to $2x + 6 = 4x - 8$?

Loop cards or dominoes

A set of dominoes or loop cards with matching items can be used in a variety of ways either as a game for a whole class or for small groups of students or in the form of a matching cards exercise to complete the loop. Such cards have a valuable self-checking element because they have to be placed in order to complete a loop with each link made correctly. The items on the cards can take many different forms: calculations and answers, words and definitions, equations and solutions, shapes and names.

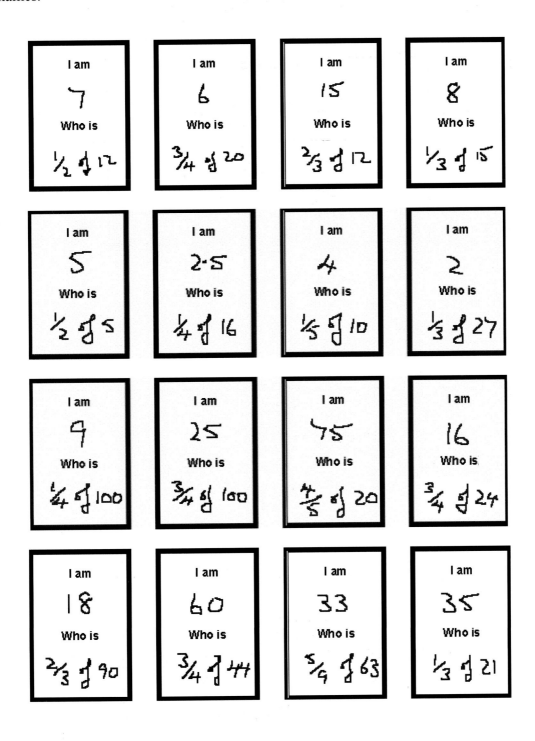

$x = 2$ $y = 4$	$x + y = 8$ $x + 2y = 11$	$x = 5$ $y = 3$	$x + y = 9$ $2x + 3y = 22$
$x = 5$ $y = 4$	$x + y = 12$ $3x + y = 22$	$x = 5$ $y = 7$	$2x + 3y = 12$ $2x + y = 8$
$x = 3$ $y = 2$	$x + 3y = 11$ $3x + y = 17$	$x = 5$ $y = 2$	$2x + 5y = 21$ $3x + 2y = 15$
$x = 3$ $y = 3$	$3x + 4y = 24$ $x + 2y = 12$	$x = 0$ $y = 6$	$2x + 5y = 29$ $3x + 7y = 42$
$x = 7$ $y = 3$	$5x + 4y = 13$ $2x + 3y = 8$	$x = 1$ $y = 2$	$3x + 5y = 26$ $5x + 2y = 18$

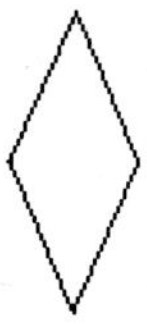

Parallelogram

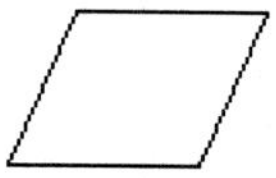

Kite

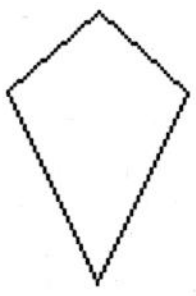

Rectangle

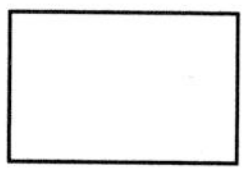

Trapezium

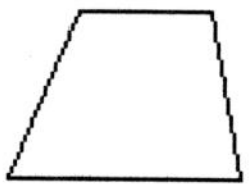

Square

Rhombus

Quadrilateral	Triangle with no equal sides.

Scalene triangle	Polygon with five equal sides and five equal angles.

Regular pentagon	Quadrilateral with at least one pair of parallel sides.

Trapezium	Rhombus with right angles.

Square	Triangle with two equal sides.

Isosceles triangle	Polygon with four sides.

$\dfrac{14}{15}$	$\dfrac{1}{2}+\dfrac{1}{3}$

$\dfrac{5}{6}$	$\dfrac{1}{4}+\dfrac{2}{5}$

$\dfrac{13}{20}$	$\dfrac{1}{2}+\dfrac{1}{6}$

$\dfrac{2}{3}$	$\dfrac{1}{5}+\dfrac{1}{3}$

$\dfrac{8}{15}$	$\dfrac{2}{5}+\dfrac{1}{3}$

$\dfrac{11}{15}$	$\dfrac{1}{6}+\dfrac{1}{3}$

$\dfrac{1}{2}$	$\dfrac{1}{5}+\dfrac{2}{3}$

$\dfrac{13}{15}$	$\dfrac{1}{3}+\dfrac{1}{4}$

$\dfrac{7}{12}$	$\dfrac{3}{4}+\dfrac{1}{8}$

$\dfrac{7}{8}$	$\dfrac{3}{5}+\dfrac{1}{3}$

Always - Sometimes - Never - Not Sure

Statements like those below can be read out or displayed to allow students, or pairs of students, to respond either on paper or with mini-whiteboards. One statement on its own may well be sufficient to promote fruitful discussion. Responses will reveal a variety of misconceptions, which provide opportunities to help students refine their thinking by encouraging them to be precise in their statements and to take account of possible exceptions or special cases.

Suppose that n is a natural number.

- $2n - 1$ is an odd number.

- $3n + 2$ is divisible by 3.

- $2n - 3$ is an even number.

- $5n - 3$ is an divisible by 2.

- $2n + 6$ is a multiple of 6.

A dialogue about one of the statements:

P: I think that $5n - 3$ is never divisible by 2.

T: Why do you think that?

P: Because 5 and 3 are odd numbers.

T: Try substituting a number for n.

P: $n = 3$ gives $15 - 3 = 12$ - that's even!

T: Is it always even then?

P: No, $n = 2$ gives $10 - 3 = 7$ and that's odd.

T: So, what can we say?

P: It's sometimes even.

T: Can you say when?

P: $5n$ has to be odd, so n has to be odd.

T: So, $5n - 3$ is even when n is odd and odd when n is even.

Consider the solutions of equations.

- Every number has two square roots.

- A quadratic equation has two different solutions.

- A cubic equation has two different solutions.

- A cubic equation has at least one solution.

- A pair of simultaneous linear equations have a single solution.

Some geometrical statements to consider.

- A trapezium is a quadrilateral.
- A quadrilateral is a parallelogram.
- The diagonals of a rectangle bisect each other.
- The diagonals of a kite are perpendicular to each other.
- The diagonals of a trapezium are equal in length.
- A square is a rhombus.
- A rhombus is a square.
- An equilateral triangle has no lines of symmetry.
- An equilateral triangle has angles of 60°.
- An isosceles triangle has two equal sides.
- An isosceles triangle has an obtuse angle.
- An isosceles triangle has two obtuse angles.

Suppose that $a > b > c$.

- $a - b$ is negative.
- $\dfrac{a}{b}$ is positive.
- c is less than a.
- $a - c = b$.
- $b = \frac{1}{2}(a + c)$.

- $\dfrac{a}{c}$ is greater than 1.
- $\dfrac{c}{b}$ is less than 0.
- a^2 is greater than b^2.
- a^3 is greater than b^3.

Suppose that x is any number (or any positive number to make it simpler):

- $x > x + 1$
- $x > x - 10$
- $x > 3x$
- $x > \dfrac{x}{3}$
- $x > 2x$

- $x^2 > 2x$
- $x^2 > 5x$
- $x^3 > x^2$
- $x > \sqrt{x}$
- $x > \dfrac{1}{x}$

Sorting tasks - Venn diagram

Ask students to place a set of numbers correctly on a Venn diagram. The first two examples use the whole numbers from 1 to 20. Varying the labels and the set of numbers sorted creates a range of possibilities. Alternatively, students can find the errors in a Venn diagram where some numbers have been placed incorrectly.

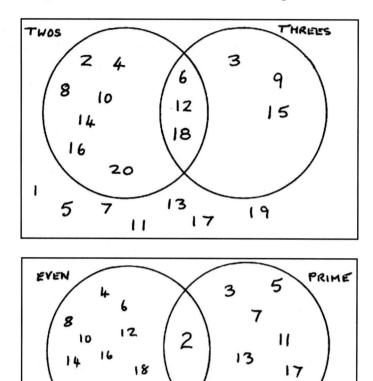

In this example, the set to be sorted consists of the twelfths from $\frac{1}{12}$ to $\frac{11}{12}$. Consider what has to change if the left hand label becomes 'less than a half'.

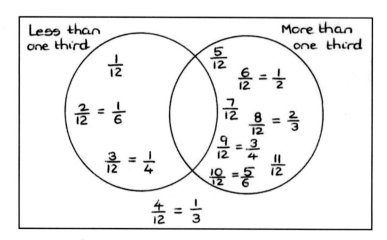

Posters to summarise key ideas and procedures.

Asking students to produce a poster to illustrate some key ideas or a solution using an important procedure provides a useful check that they are making sense of ideas from a lesson. This provides an appropriate task towards the end of a lesson or for homework.

Writing out a single solution with full details of the steps, as with the equation below, as something to be displayed on the classroom wall, will encourage students to check carefully what they are writing and will reveal misunderstandings. Similarly, asking students to produce a poster to illustrate the meaning of some key words will reinforce their knowledge and reveal any confusion.

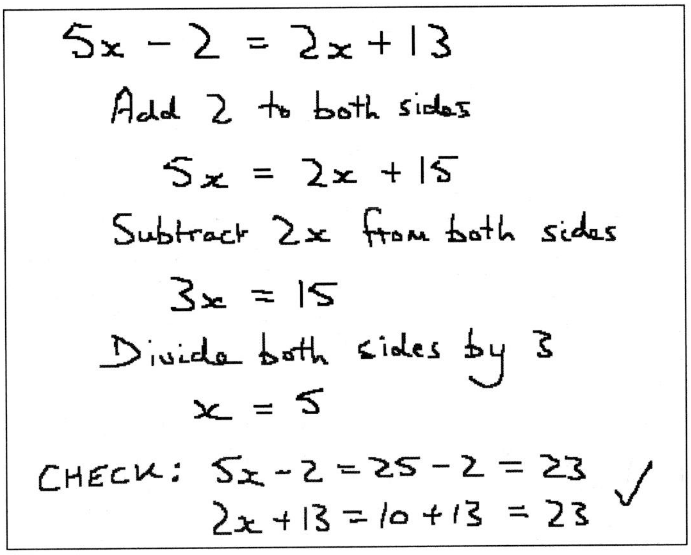

5x − 2 = 2x + 13
Add 2 to both sides
5x = 2x + 15
Subtract 2x from both sides
3x = 15
Divide both sides by 3
x = 5
CHECK: 5x − 2 = 25 − 2 = 23
2x + 13 = 10 + 13 = 23

How do you find and check the solution of an equation?

CHORD
DIAMETER
RADIUS
CIRCUMFERENCE

What are the key words related to circles?

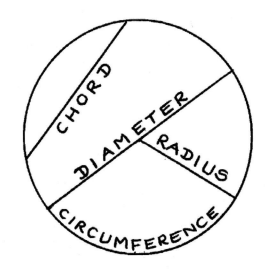

```
X 2   DOUBLE
X 4   DOUBLE  DOUBLE
X 8   DOUBLE, DOUBLE, DOUBLE
X 16  DOUBLE, . . . . . . . ?
```

What quick ways for multiplying have you learnt today?

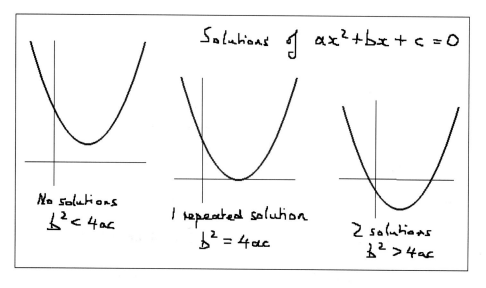

What have you learnt about the solutions of quadratic equations?

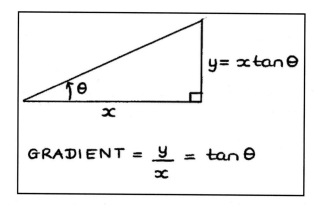

What have you learnt about tangents today?

Topic-based Classroom Resources: Number

Larger, Smaller or Equal?

- $5+3$ or $3+5$
- 5×3 or 3×5
- $5-3$ or $3-5$
- $5\div3$ or $3\div5$
- $20\div2$ or $20\div3$
- ½ of ¼ or ¼ of ½
- $20\div$ ½ or $20\div$ ⅓
- 2^5 or 5^2
- 2^2 or 3^2
- $\sqrt{49}$ or 10% of 60
- 2^3 or 3^2
- ½ of 40 or $40\div$ ½
- ¼ of 16 or ⅓ of 15
- 0.1^2 or 0.1^3
- ¼$\times16$ or $16\times$¼
- 1^5 or 1^{10}
- 2/5 or 0.25
- ⅜ of 5 or ⅝ of 3
- 0.35 or 0.4
- 15% of 40 or 10% or 55
- 2.7×4 or 27×0.04
- 2.7×4 or 0.27×40
- 15% of 20 or 20% or 15
- $40\div2$ or $40\times$ ½

- The sum of the factors of 6 **or** the sum of the factors of 9.

- The sum of the first 4 odd numbers **or** the sum of the first 4 even numbers.

- The sum of the first 100 odd numbers **or** the sum of the first 100 even numbers.

- The sum of the squares of 3 and 4 **or** the square of the sum of the same two numbers.

- The product of the squares of 3 and 4 **or** the square of the product of the same two numbers.

- The reciprocal of the sum of 2 and 3 **or** the sum of the reciprocals of the same two numbers.

The important thing here is to ask students to justify their responses regardless of whether they are right or wrong. That provides evidence about their thinking and opportunities to discuss the inevitable misconceptions and also to compare alternative approaches. Asking students to make up their own questions is also a revealing task which will provide further insights into their thinking and opportunities for discussion.

Using a Number Line

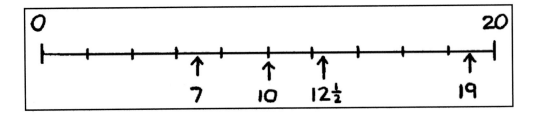

Label the end points with 0 and 20. Insert 10, 7, 19 and $12\frac{1}{2}$ correctly.

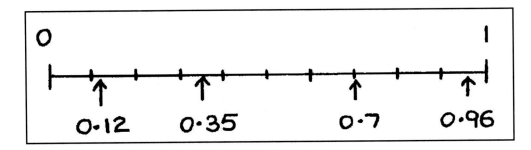

Label the end points with 0 and 1. Insert 0.7, 0.35, 0.12 and 0.96 correctly.

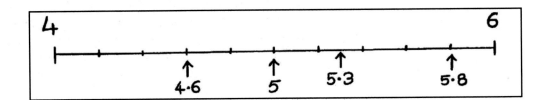

Label the end points with 4 and 6. Place 5, 5.8, 4.6 and 5.3 correctly.

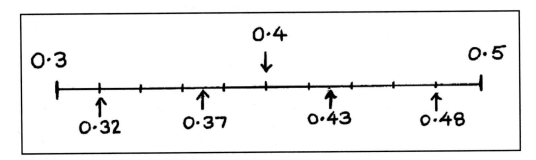

Label the end points with 0.3 and 0.5. Place 0.4, 0.43, 0.32, 0.37 and 0.48 correctly.

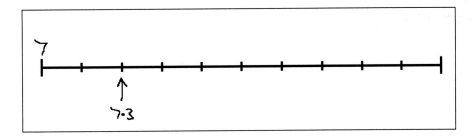

What is the other end point?

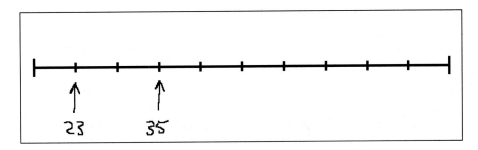

What are the two end points?

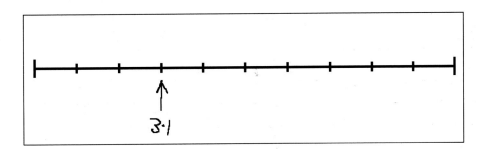

What could the two end points be?

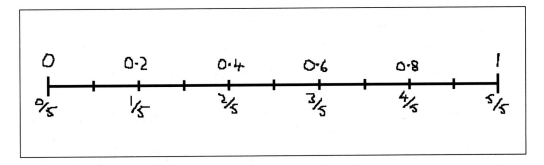

Label the end points with 0 and 1. Calculate $\frac{1}{5}, \frac{2}{5}, \frac{3}{5}$ and $\frac{4}{5}$ as decimals and insert them in their correct positions on the line. Repeat with other sets of fractions.

Number in a Box

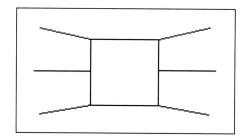

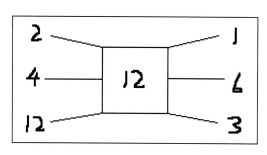

Place a number in the box and ask students to give some factors of that number.

Replace the number in the box with 24 or 6 or 600.

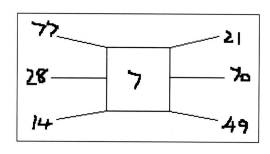

Place a number in the box and ask students to give some multiples of that number.

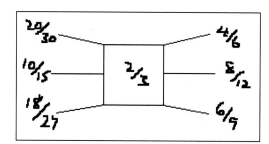

Place a fraction in the box and ask students to give some equivalent fractions.

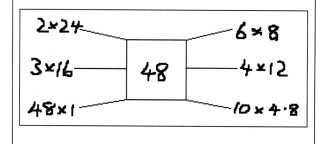

Place a number in the box and ask students to give some equivalent products.

Fractions in a Bag

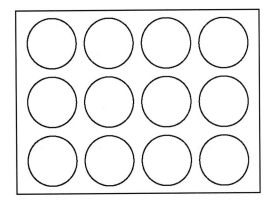

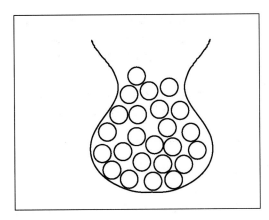 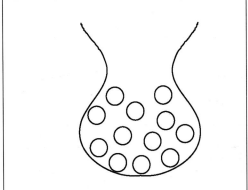

Use one of the diagrams above:

- Shade $\frac{2}{3}$ of the balls.
- What fraction of the balls remain unshaded?

- If I take one ball out, what fraction is now shaded?

- Is the fraction the same whichever ball is taken out?

- What happens to the fractions if an extra ball is put in?

- Shade $\frac{1}{2}$ of the balls in blue.

- Shade $\frac{1}{3}$ of the balls in red.

- What fraction is now shaded?

- What fraction remains unshaded?

Fraction Bricks

Each fraction is the sum of the two fractions below.

Give three fractions across the bottom row.

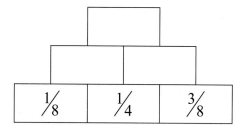 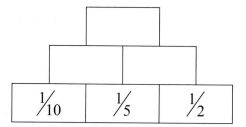

For more challenging problems start with 1 at the top and find fractions to fit.

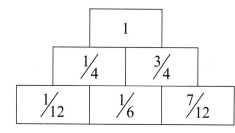 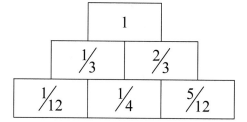

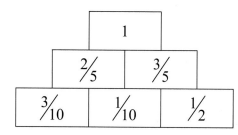 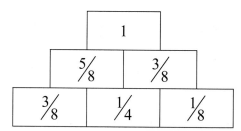

Try the same ideas with decimals:

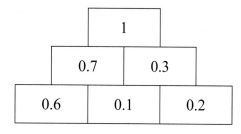 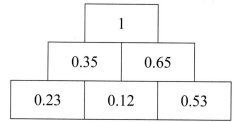

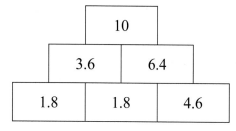 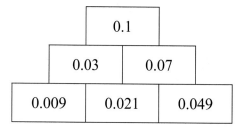

Topic-based Classroom Resources: Algebra

Understanding Expressions

- Write an expression for 3 more than a number a.

- Write an expression for 3 less than a number a.

| $a + 3$ | $3 + a$ | $a - 3$ | $3 - a$ |

Points for discussion.

- How can we check if $a + 3$ the same as $3 + a$? What happens with $a = 2$? Try some other numbers.

- Does it matter if different people write expressions in different ways. We normally put the letter first, but there is nothing incorrect about writing $3 + a$. With multiplication, by convention we write $3a$ rather than $a3$.

- Is $a - 3$ the same as $3 - a$ with $a = 2$? Try some other numbers.

- What does $a - 3$ mean? How else can we say it?

- What does $3 - a$ mean? How else can we say it?

Write an expression for a number b multiplied by itself.

| b^2 | $2b$ | bb | $b \times b$ |

Points to consider.

- Is b^2 the same as $2b$ with $b = 3$? Try some other numbers.

- Why is it better to write b^2 rather than bb? Index notation is clearly better for something like b^8! However, bb is similar to the way we write an expression like ab.

- We need to distinguish clearly between what is **wrong** and what is **conventional** in the way expressions are written.

Understanding Expressions

Either display some cards like these or write the expressions on the board.

$$\boxed{n} \quad \boxed{n^2} \quad \boxed{n+n} \quad \boxed{2n} \quad \boxed{2+n} \quad \boxed{n \div 2}$$

$$\boxed{2n-n} \quad \boxed{n+2} \quad \boxed{n-2}$$

1. Which expression is always the same as $\dfrac{n}{2}$?

2. Which expression is always the same as $n \times n$?

3. Which two expressions are always the same as $2 \times n$?

4. Write a new expression that is always the same as $3n + 2n$.

5. Write down three pairs of expressions which are equivalent.

6. If n is an integer, which expressions will always have an even value?

7. Which two expressions add together to give $4n$?

8. Which three expressions add together to give $4n$?

9. Which two expressions add together to give $2n + 4$?

10. Which two expressions differ by 4?

Points to consider.

- Equivalence: illustrate by substituting values.

- Conventions: how do you normally write $n \times n$ and $2 \times n$?

- Odd or even: how do you tell?

- Write a new card: what questions can be asked?

- Ask students to produce a new set of cards and a set of questions to go with them.

Understanding Expressions

$$0.8n \qquad n^2 \qquad \sqrt{n} \qquad \frac{n}{0.8} \qquad \frac{1}{n}$$

For each expression n can be any positive integer.

- Which expression will always be less than n?

- Which expression will always be greater than n?

- When $n = 1$, which expressions have a value of 1?

- If $n = 1$, which expression has a value greater than 1?

- If $n = 1$, which expression has a value less than 1?

- When $n = 4$, which expressions have a value less than 4?

- If $n = 10$, which expression will have the smallest value?

- Which expression and which value of n would give a value of 100?

- Which expression and which value of n would give a value of 7?

- Which expression will never give an answer greater than 1?

- Which expression will always give a value that is an integer?

- As n gets bigger which expression gets smaller?

Points to consider.

- What happens, where appropriate, if n is a negative integer?

- What happens, where appropriate, if n takes fractional values?

Forming Expressions

Questions to ask with responses displayed on mini-whiteboards.

- I start with x. I multiply by 2 and add 7. What do I get?

- I start with m. I add 3 then multiply by 5. What do I have now?

  Discuss the equivalence of $5(m+3)$ and $5m+15$.

- I start with y. I subtract 10 and then divide by 4. What do I have now?

  Discuss $\dfrac{y-10}{4}$ and $\dfrac{1}{4}(y-10)$.

- I start with c. I add 9 and square the result. I divide by 5, then take the square root, then double the answer. What do I have now?

  This should be read slowly (twice) with students amending their expression at each stage.

- Think of a number. Add 3. Double the result. Then subtract 6. Then halve the result. What do you get?

  Students get different results but they should be the values which they chose originally. Re-read the instructions with students testing out another value (which could be a much larger number or a fraction or decimal or negative number). Then repeat the process with students starting with x, to show what is happening.

  $$x \;\rightarrow\; x+3 \;\rightarrow\; 2x+6 \;(\text{or } 2(x+3)) \;\rightarrow\; 2x \;\rightarrow\; x$$

- Think of a number. Double it. Double it again. Subtract 4. Divide by 4. Add 1.

  Again try this with various numbers, then with x.

  $$x \;\rightarrow\; 2x \;\rightarrow\; 4x \;\rightarrow\; 4x-4 \;\rightarrow\; x-1 \;\rightarrow\; x$$

- Think of a number. Square it. Double the result. Add 10. Halve the result. Subtract 5. What is the square root of your answer?

  $$a \;\rightarrow\; a^2 \;\rightarrow\; 2a^2 \;\rightarrow\; 2a^2+10 \;\rightarrow\; a^2+5 \;\rightarrow\; a^2 \;\rightarrow\; a \;(\text{or} -a)$$

Understanding Expressions: Divisibility

$2n-1$	$2n+4$	$3n$

$2n+3$	$3n-1$	$3n+2$

Preliminary task: students, individually or in pairs, generate the first five numbers of the sequences given by each expression.

Sort the six expressions into three groups in response to the questions.

ALWAYS	SOMETIMES	NEVER
$2n+4$	$3n$ $3n-1$ $3n+2$	$2n-1$ $2n+3$

- If n is an integer, when are these expressions divisible by 2?

- How do you explain the choice of column for each example?

ALWAYS	SOMETIMES	NEVER
$3n$	$2n+4$ $2n-1$ $2n+3$	$3n-1$ $3n+2$

- If n is an integer, when are these expressions divisible by 3?

- How do you explain the choice of column for each example?

53

Things to do and discuss:

- As an alternative, display one expression and ask students to respond with 'always', 'sometimes' or 'never'.

- What happens if you add 2 even numbers or 3 even numbers or lots of even numbers?

- What happens if you add 2 odd numbers or 3 odd numbers or lots of odd numbers?

- What happens if you add a mixture of odd and even numbers? When will the result be odd and when will it be even?

- What happens if you add a constant to a set of multiples?

- Why do some linear sequences alternate between odd and even?

- Try generating sequences on a graphical calculator as follows:

$$\text{ENTER } 3 \ \rightarrow \ \text{ADD } 2 \ \rightarrow \ \text{ENTER} \ \rightarrow \ \text{ENTER} \ \rightarrow \ \dots\dots$$

- Generating sequences on a spreadsheet reinforces the meaning and purpose of expressions as a way of defining sequences. Observing the effect of varying the values of the variable as shown in the illustrations below is particularly instructive in reinforcing understanding of how particular sequences behave.

n	2n-1	2n+4	3n	2n+3	3n-1	3n+2
1	1	6	3	5	2	5
2	3	8	6	7	5	8
3	5	10	9	9	8	11
4	7	12	12	11	11	14
5	9	14	15	13	14	17

n	2n-1	2n+4	3n	2n+3	3n-1	3n+2
57	113	118	171	117	170	173
58	115	120	174	119	173	176
59	117	122	177	121	176	179
60	119	124	180	123	179	182
61	121	126	183	125	182	185

Expanding and Factorising Quadratic Expressions

Expanding: five choices displayed.

A	$x^2 - 3x + 4$
B	$x^2 - 3x - 4$
C	$x^2 + 3x - 4$
D	$x^2 - 4$
E	None of these

Ask students to give the letter corresponding to the expanded form of each of the following.

$(x-1)(x+5)$	$(x-2)(x+2)$	$(x-2)^2$
$(x-4)(x+1)$	$(x+1)(x-4)$	$(x-1)(x+4)$

Factorising: five choices displayed.

A	$(x-1)(x+3)$
B	$(x+1)(x+3)$
C	$(x-1)(x-3)$
D	$(x+1)(x-3)$
E	None of these

Ask students to give the letter corresponding to the factorised form of each of the following.

$x^2 + 4x + 3$	$x^2 - 2x - 3$	$x^2 + 2x + 3$
$x^2 + 2x - 3$	$x^2 - 4x - 3$	$x^2 - 4x + 3$

Graphs of Linear Functions

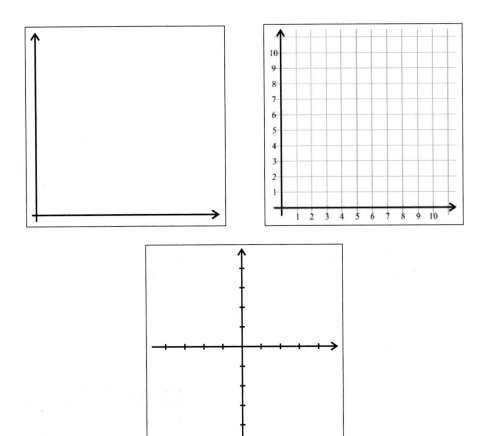

Ask students either to **sketch** on axes without a grid or **plot** on axes with a grid a variety of straight lines. These should be grouped carefully to demonstrate the effect of changing the gradient and y-intercept.

$$x = 2, \quad x = 4, \quad x = {}^-1, \quad x = {}^-3, \quad x = 0$$

$$y = 2, \quad y = 4, \quad y = {}^-1, \quad y = {}^-3, \quad y = 0$$

$$y = x, \quad y = 2x, \quad y = 3x, \quad y = {}^-x, \quad y = {}^-2x$$

$$y = x, \quad y = x+1, \quad y = x+2, \quad y = x-1, \quad y = x-2$$

$$y = 2x, \quad y = 2x+1, \quad y = 2x+2, \quad y = 2x-1, \quad y = 2x-2$$

$$y = {}^-x, \quad y = 3-x, \quad y = 5-x, \quad y = 8-x, \quad y = {}^-3-x$$

$$x+y = 0, \quad x+y = 3, \quad x+y = 5, \quad x+y = 8, \quad x+y = {}^-3$$

Simplifying Linear Expressions

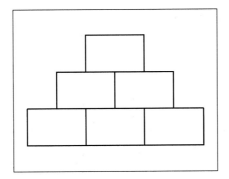

Bricks (or pyramids) can be used on mini-whiteboards or as pencil and paper tasks. They can provide rapid feedback as to whether students have mastered a particular skill. Errors can be used as a focus for discussion which can be followed up readily with a further question to check whether the difficulty has been overcome.

Starting with expressions in the bricks in the bottom row, the other expressions are obtained by **adding** the expressions in the pair of bricks below.

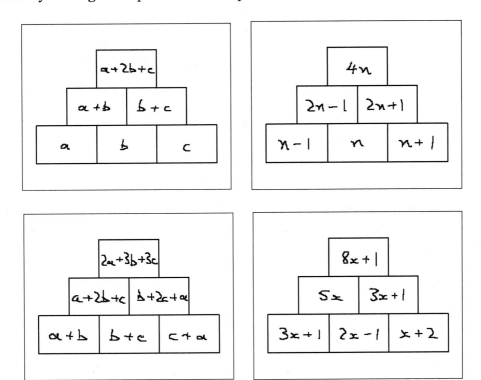

It is useful to compare what happens with sets of numbers corresponding to the different examples. In each case the expression in the top brick enables you to predict the number that will appear in that position when three numbers are placed in the bottom row. In the first example, three random numbers are chosen, whereas in the second example the three numbers are consecutive resulting in a top number which is always four times the middle number in the bottom row.

As an alternative, the expressions may be obtained by **subtracting** or **multiplying** the pair of expressions below.

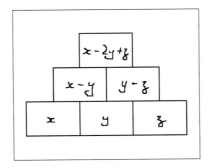
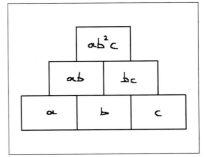

Different challenges are provided by varying the positions of the three initial expressions. Expressions can be given in any of the combinations shown below by the highlighted rectangles, which have been organised into levels of difficulty.

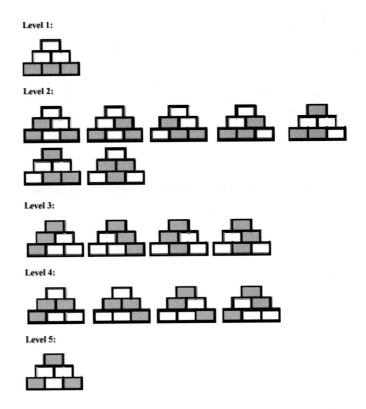

A more open-ended challenge is provided by giving students an expression to place in the top brick and then asking them to find expressions for the other bricks.

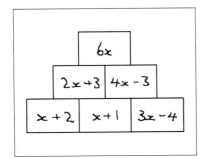
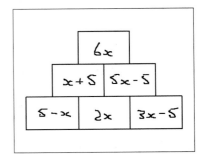

Topic-based Classroom Resources: Geometry

Symmetry

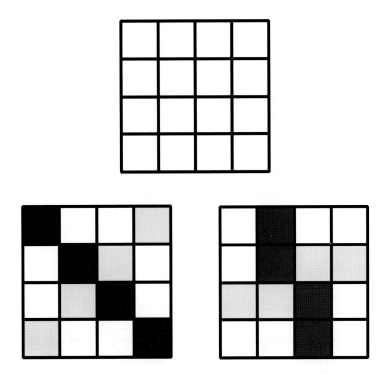

Display pictures and ask students to describe the symmetry in detail.

With a blank grid, ask students to shade in two or more squares so that the grid has:

- one vertical line of symmetry;

- one diagonal line of symmetry;

- one horizontal and one vertical line of symmetry;

- two diagonal lines of symmetry;

- four lines of symmetry.

Ask similar questions with rotational symmetry.

What happens if two colours or types of shading are allowed?

Consider what happens if the number of squares to be shaded is specified.

- What symmetries are possible if only six squares are shaded?

- What symmetries are possible if an odd number of squares is shaded?

Parallel Lines

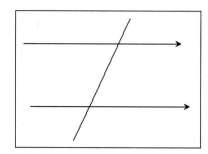

Draw a pair of parallel lines and a transversal.

- Mark a pair of corresponding angles.

- Mark a pair of alternate angles.

- Mark a pair of vertically opposite angles.

- Mark a pair of supplementary angles.

- Indicate one angle on the diagram and label it as *a*. Ask students to mark on their diagrams all the angles that are equal to *a*.

Ask students to discuss their reasoning using appropriate vocabulary: parallel, transversal, corresponding, alternate, vertically opposite.

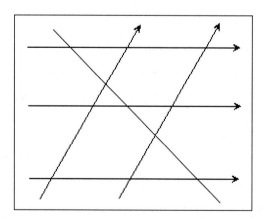

- How many lines are there here?   • How many triangles can you see?

- How many intersections?   • How many trapezia?

- How many sets of parallel lines?   • How many parallelograms?

Ask the same set of questions as for the first diagram.

Angles on a Clock Face

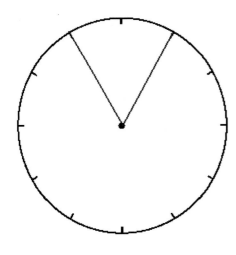

Show students an angle:

- Draw an angle of the same size.

- Draw another angle of the same size.

- How many degrees is the angle?

Show them another angle:

- Draw another angle of the same size.

- How many degrees is the angle?

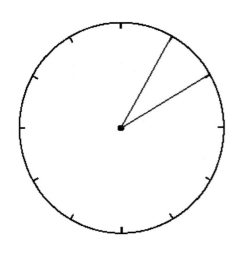

Ask students to draw angles:

- Show me an angle of 90º.

- Show me an angle of 30º.

- Show me another angle of 30º.

- Show me an angle of 60º.

- Show me an angle of 45º.

- Show me an angle of 120º.

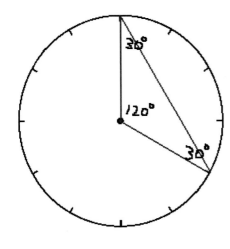

Show them an angle:

- Draw another angle of the same size.

- How many degrees is the angle?

Join the tips of the angle:

- Show me.

- What type of triangle is it?

- How many degrees are the other angles?

Questions about Polygons

- What do we call any many-sided two-dimensional shape?

- What is the name for five-sided shapes?
  Link to pentathlon, pentagram, Pentateuch …

- How many sides does a decagon have?
  Link to decimal, decade, decathlon …

- How many sides does a heptagon have?
  Link to heptathlon and 'sept' as seven in French and September (originally the seventh month in the Roman calendar)

- If a shape has all its sides equal and all its angles equal, how do we describe it?

- Sketch a regular hexagon.

- How many lines of symmetry does a regular hexagon have?

- What is the order of rotational symmetry of a regular hexagon?

- Sketch an irregular hexagon. Sketch some more.

- Sketch a re-entrant (concave) hexagon.

- Sketch a pentagon with a pair of equal parallel sides.

- What is the name for any eight-sided shape?

- What shape is a 50p or 20p coin?
  A regular curved heptagon – each arc is centred at the opposite vertex as shown in the diagram below.

- Why is the diameter of the curved heptagon constant?

- What is the perimeter of a regular curved heptagon in terms of the diameter?

- How does it compare with the circumference of a circle with the same diameter?

Representing Three-dimensional Objects

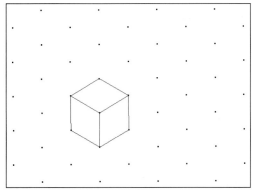 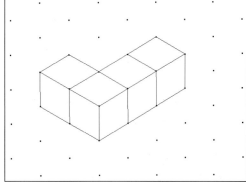

An isometric grid is an ideal resource for introducing students to drawing two-dimensional representations of three-dimensional shapes, but do note that it must be made clear to students whether the grid is to be arranged in landscape or portrait view.

With a whiteboard grid it is not a problem if they make mistakes because it is so easy to change things. Start with a simple cube with edges of unit length, and then ask them to build up other configurations with cubes and larger cubes or cuboids with edges of different lengths.

- Draw a single cube.

- How many faces can you see? How many faces are hidden?

- How many vertices can you see? How many vertices are hidden?

- How many edges can you see? How many edges are hidden?

- Draw a cube behind and to the left of the first one.

- Draw a cube behind and to the right of the first one.

- Draw another cube to the right of that.

- Answer the same questions about the faces, vertices and edges.

- Sketch a triangular prism.

- How many faces, vertices and edges does a triangular prism have?

- How many planes of symmetry could a triangular prism have?

- What do we usually call a circular prism?

- How many planes of symmetry does a cylinder have?

- Sketch a tetrahedron.

- How many faces, vertices and edges does a tetrahedron have?

- How many faces, vertices and edges does an octahedron have?

- How many planes of symmetry does a cuboid have in general?

- How many planes of symmetry does a cube have?

Properties of Circles

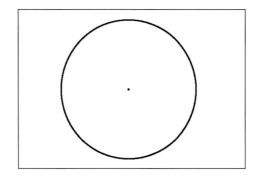

Use a whiteboard displaying a circle.

- Draw a straight line from the centre to the circumference. What is the line called?

- Draw two straight lines from the centre to the circumference. Join the two points on the circumference to make a triangle. Mark two equal lengths. Mark two equal angles. What kind of triangle is it?

- Draw a chord. Join both ends of the chord to the centre of the circle. What kind of triangle is it?

- Draw a diameter. Join each of the ends of the diameter with straight lines to any point on the circumference of the circle. What do you notice?

- Draw two perpendicular diameters. Join the ends of the diameters to make a quadrilateral. What kind of quadrilateral is it?

- Draw two diameters that are not perpendicular. Join the ends of the diameters to make a quadrilateral. What can you say about the quadrilateral?

- Mark any four points on the circumference and join them to make a four sided shape. Name the shape. Draw the diagonals. Mark a pair of equal angles. Why are the angles equal?

- Draw a chord. Draw a line to show the shortest distance from the centre of the circle to the chord. What do you notice about the line?

- Choose a point on your page outside the circle and draw a tangent from that point to the circle. From the same point draw another tangent to the circle. Join the two points of contact to the centre of the circle. What kind of quadrilateral is formed?

Vocabulary of the circle.

- Diameter, radius, arc, chord, sector, segment, semicircle, quadrant, circumference, tangent, cyclic quadrilateral, major and minor arc, major and minor sector and major and minor segment.

Angles in Circles

Mark 5 points A, B, C, D and O on a blank clock face as shown.

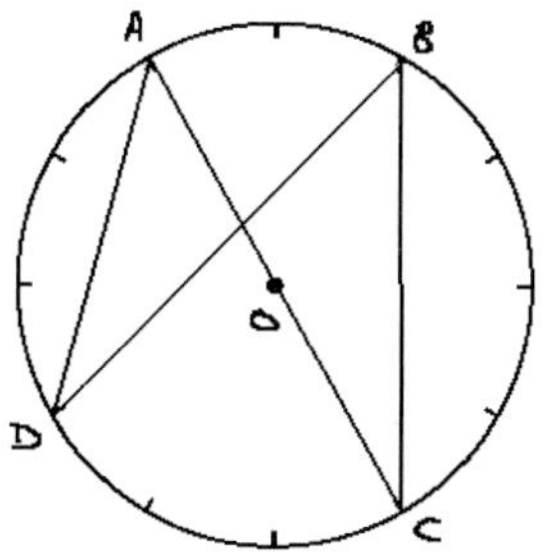	Mark an angle equal to angle *CAD*. Mark an angle equal to angle *ADB*. Mark two other equal angles. What can you say about the two triangles in the diagram?
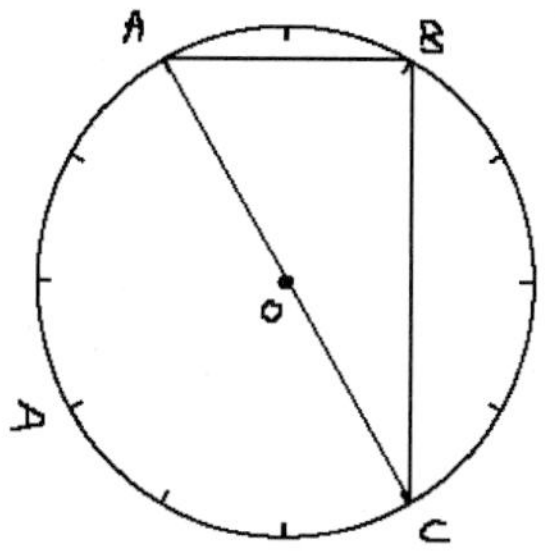	How many degrees is angle *ABC*? Why is angle *AOB* equal to 60°? Why is *AB* equal in length to *AO*? How many degrees is angle *ACB*?
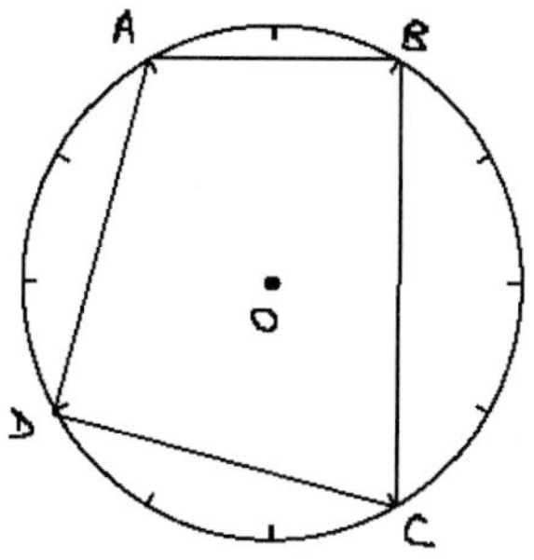	What is the name given to the quadrilateral *ABCD*? How many degrees are there in each of angles *ABC* and *ADC*? If angle *BCD* is 75°, how many degrees is angle *BAD*?
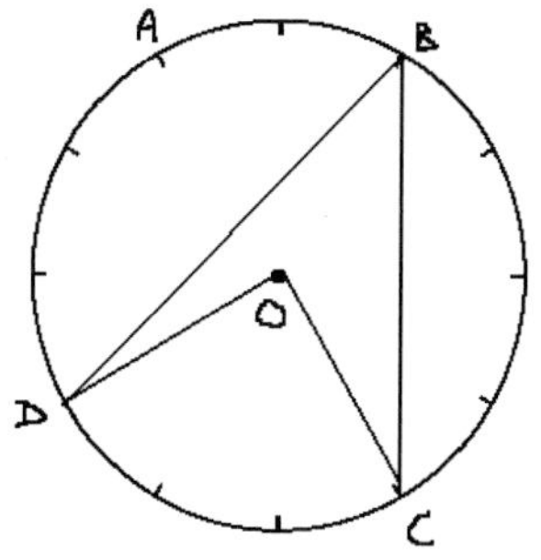	How is angle *COD* related to angle *CBD*? How many degrees is angle *COD*? How many degrees is angle *CBD*? How many degrees is angle *CAD*?
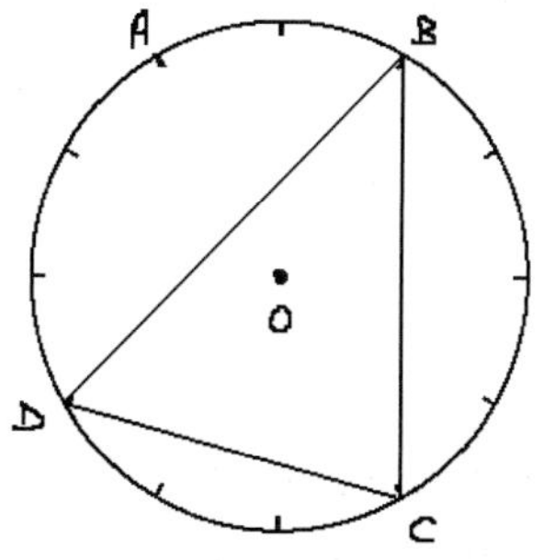	How many degrees are there in each of the angles of triangle *BCD*? How many degrees are there in each of the angles of triangle *ACD*? What is the ratio of the three angles of triangle *BCD*?

Topic-based Classroom Resources: Probability and Statistics

Probabilities with Matching Cards

$\dfrac{3}{13}$	$\dfrac{1}{4}$	$\dfrac{1}{2}$	$\dfrac{2}{13}$

$\dfrac{1}{52}$	$\dfrac{1}{13}$	$\dfrac{3}{4}$	$\dfrac{1}{26}$

Give students in groups sets of cards which display probabilities as shown above. Ask them to show the appropriate card when you ask a question.

If you select a card from an ordinary pack (no jokers!), what is the probability of getting:

a heart?	a six?	a picture card?	not a red card?
a jack?	not a spade?	a king?	a red five?
a black card?	six of clubs?	a black ace?	a five or a six?

Alternatively, give them the set of questions on cards and ask them to show the appropriate card (or cards) when you show them one of the probability cards.

A further alternative is to give them both sets of cards and ask them to match them up. Of course, some questions have the same answer!

A more revealing task is to ask them to make up a set of questions for a given set of probabilities.

Probabilities on a Number Line

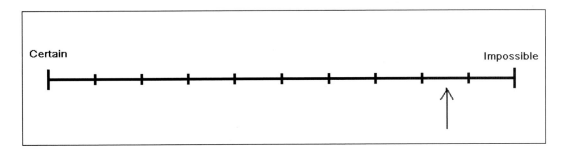

Ask students to label a number line with 'impossible' and 'certain' at the ends.

Ask them to place an arrow on the number line to denote the probability of events.

Ask their reasons for their response to each question.

How likely is:

- a head when you spin a fair coin;

- a red card when you cut a pack of cards;

- a rainy day tomorrow;

- Coventry City winning the FA Cup next season;

- a six when you throw a dice;

- two sixes when you throw two dice;

- tomorrow is Wednesday;

- my birthday is tomorrow;

- an odd number when you throw a dice;

- a number less than 3 when you throw a dice;

- a number more than 3 when you throw a dice;

- meeting an elephant on the way home;

- being late for school tomorrow;

- living to be 100.

Probability with Balls in a Bag

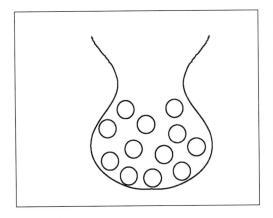 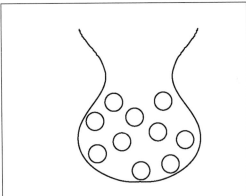

Left-hand diagram (a bag with 12 balls)

Ask students to shade an appropriate number of balls in the bag so that the probability of picking a shaded ball is:

$$\frac{1}{4}, \quad \frac{1}{12}, \quad \frac{1}{2}, \quad \frac{3}{4}, \quad \frac{1}{3}, \quad \frac{1}{6}, \quad \frac{5}{6}, \quad \frac{7}{12}$$

Right-hand diagram (a bag with 10 balls)

Ask students to shade an appropriate number of balls in the bag so that the probability of picking a shaded ball is:

$$\frac{1}{10}, \quad \frac{7}{10}, \quad \frac{1}{2}, \quad \frac{1}{5}, \quad \frac{9}{10}, \quad 1, \quad \frac{3}{5}, \quad \frac{4}{5}$$

Reverse the problem – show them a diagram with a number of shaded balls. Ask for the probability. Change the number of shaded balls.

Shade the balls with some red and some blue. Ask them the probability of randomly choosing:

a red ball	a ball that is not red	a ball that is either blue or red	a ball that is not blue
a ball that is neither blue nor red	a blue ball	a ball that is both red and blue	a ball that is round

68

Using a bag with 24 balls.

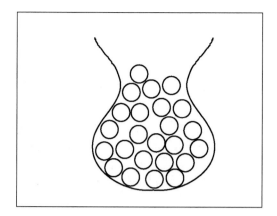

Students shade any six balls.

What is the probability of selecting at random a shaded ball from the bag?

Can you simplify your answer?

What is the probability of selecting at random an unshaded ball?

What is the ratio of shaded balls to unshaded balls in the bag?

Can your answer be simplified?

Now shade two more of the balls in the bag and repeat the questions above.

Now shade enough balls so that it becomes:

- Equally likely that you will select at random a shaded or unshaded ball;

- Twice as likely that you will select at random a shaded ball as an unshaded ball.

If you now add one extra ball, what is the probability of selecting this additional ball at random from the bag?

Points to consider:

- Finding the probabilities:

- Simplifying fractions and ratios;

- Equivalent fractions;

- Relationships between proportions and ratios.

Probability

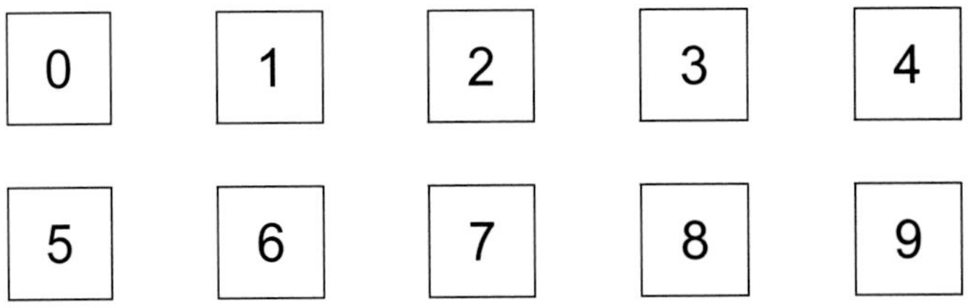

0	1	2	3	4
5	6	7	8	9

Ten digit cards are placed in a hat and selected at random without replacement. The task is to place them so as to give the biggest or smallest answer to the calculation when all the boxes have been filled. Once a number has been placed in a box it may not be moved, so the chances of suitable numbers appearing at each stage have to be considered. *Games in the Teaching of Mathematics* by Kirkby (1992) is a good source of ideas of this type.

Addition

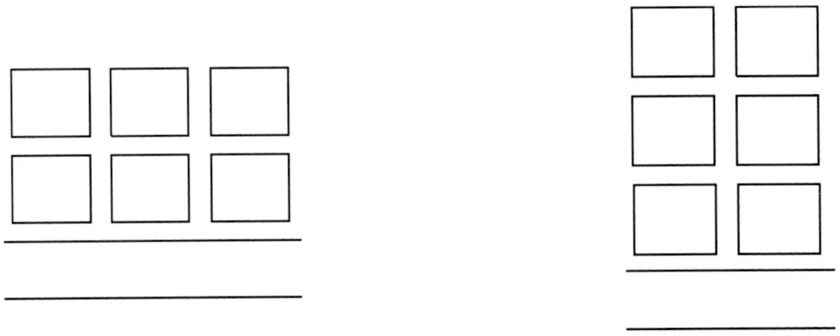

Subtraction

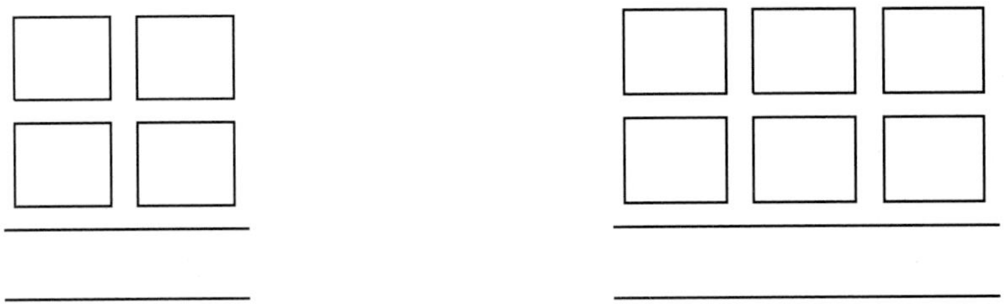

Multiplication

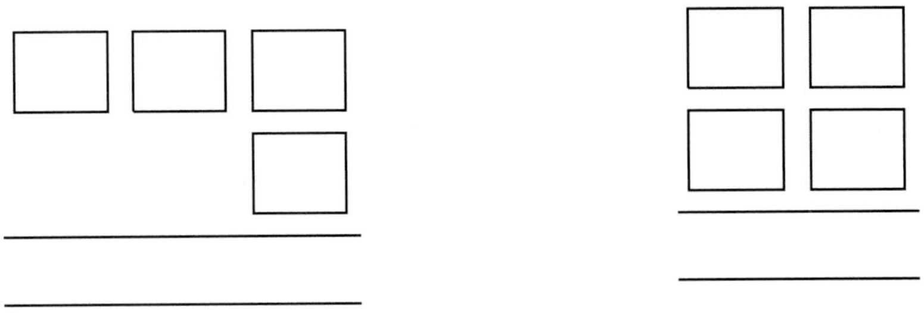

Points to consider.

- The importance of place value.

- Probability linked to the best strategy for placing each digit.

- What determines how to make the difference biggest or smallest?

- Deciding, without a calculator, which product is bigger: 73×52 or 72×53.

Bar Charts

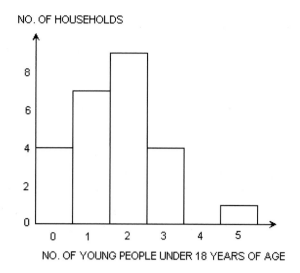

NO. OF HOUSEHOLDS

NO. OF YOUNG PEOPLE UNDER 18 YEARS OF AGE

- Tell me something you can work out from the bar chart.

- How many households are there altogether?

- Which number of young people occurs most often?

- What is the special name given to that number?

- How many households have no young people?

- What percentage of households has no young people?

- How many households have more than two young people?

- What percentage of households has more than two young people?

- What percentage of households has fewer than two young people?

- What percentage of households has just two young people?

- How many young people are there altogether in the households that have just two?

- How many young people are there altogether?

- How do you calculate the mean number of young people per household?

- If the households with no young people were excluded, would the mean be bigger or smaller?

- If one family with two young people moves away and is replaced by a family with three young people, would the mean be bigger or smaller?

The Mean

- Write down the five numbers 7, 5, 3, 9, 1. Find the mean, median and range.

- Repeat with 5, 2, 11, 2, 10.

- Write down five numbers between 0 and 100 with a mean of 40.

36, 38, 40, 42, 44 *2 above 2 below; 4 above and 4 below.*

40, 23, 57, 10, 70 *23 is 17 below 40, 57 is 17 above. Likewise with 10 and 70.*

13, 52, 48, 27, 60 *Write down four numbers. Find a fifth number so the total is 200. Why 200?*

10, 20, 30, 40, 100 *The same idea with easy numbers. The sum of the first four has to be 100.*

40, 40, 40, 40, 40 *The simplest example of all!*

Some variations:

- Include at least one zero.

- Make the first number 0 and last number 100.

- Include the maximum possible number of zeros.

- Find five numbers so that only one is 'above average' (above the mean).

20, 20, 30, 30, 100

- Find five numbers so that only one is 'below average' (below the mean).

10, 45, 45, 50, 50

- Include one more number in the current list so that the mean remains at 40.

10, 45, 45, 50, 50, 40

- Change a number so that the mean becomes greater than 40.

- Change a number so that the mean becomes less than 40.

Links to geometry:

- Plot two points: (1, 3) and (5, 7). Find the mean of the x coordinates and the mean of the y coordinates. Plot these as a new point. What happens?

- Plot three points: (1, 3), (5, 7) and (3, 2). Find the mean of the x coordinates and the mean of the y coordinates. Plot these as a new point. What happens?

Bibliography

Askew, S. and Lodge, C. (2000) 'Gifts, ping-pong and loops – linking feedback and learning' in Askew, S. (ed) *Feedback for Learning* London: Routledge

Assessment Reform Group (1999) *Assessment for Learning: Beyond the Black Box* University of Cambridge School of Education
Available at: http://arg.educ.cam.ac.uk

Assessment Reform Group (2002) *Assessment for Learning: 10 Principles*
Available at: http://arg.educ.cam.ac.uk

Black, Paul and Wiliam, Dylan (1998) *Inside the Black Box. Raising Standards through Classroom Assessment*   London: King's College
Available at: http://www.kiva.net/~pdkintl/kappan/kbla9810.htm

Black, P., Harrison, C., Lee, C., Marshall, B. and Wiliam, D. (2002) *Working inside the Black Box. Assessment for learning in the classroom* London: NferNelson

Butler, Ruth (1988) 'Enhancing and undermining intrinsic motivation: the effects of task-involving and ego-involving education on interest and performance' in *British Journal of Psychology*, Volume 58, pp.1-14

DfES (2004) *Key Stage 3 National Strategy Assessment for Learning: Guidance for School Leaders*   Reference: DfES 0043 2004G

Gabb, Jane (2000) 'Support through Questioning' in *Equals*, Vol.6, no. 3

Holt, John (1958) *How Children Fail*   Penguin Books

Kirkby, Dave (1992) *Games in the Teaching of Mathematics*
Cambridge University Press

Lee, Clare (2001) 'Using Assessment for Effective Learning' in *Mathematics Teaching*, 175, June 2001

Mathematical Association (1992) *Mental Methods in Mathematics : A First Resort*

Mathematical Association (2002) *Position Paper on Assessment*
Available at: http://www.m-a.org.uk/docs/library/2033.doc

Ofsted (2003) *Good Assessment Practice in Mathematics*
Reference: HMI 1477

Ofsted (2005) *Ofsted Subject Reports 2003/04: Mathematics in Secondary Schools*
Reference: HMI 2326

QCA (2003) *Assessment for Learning: Using Assessment to Raise Achievement in Mathematics* Reference: QCA/03/1070

Ronayne, Michael (1999) 'Marking and Feedback' in *Improving Schools*, Vol.2, no.2 Available at: http://www.tta.gov.uk/php/read.php?sectionid=82&articleid=689

Stigler, James W. and Hiebert, James (1997) 'Understanding and Improving Classroom Instruction: an Overview of the TIMSS Study' in *Phi Delta Kappan* September 1997 Available at: http://www.pdkintl.org/kappan/kstg9709.htm

The following three articles appear in the appendix:

Wiliam, Dylan (1999a) 'Formative Assessment in Mathematics Part 1: Rich Questioning' in *Equals*, Vol.5, no. 2 (1999) The Mathematical Association

Wiliam, Dylan (1999b) 'Formative Assessment in Mathematics Part 2: Feedback' in *Equals*, Vol.5, no. 3 The Mathematical Association

Wiliam, Dylan (2000) 'Formative Assessment in Mathematics Part 3: The Learner's Role' in *Equals*, Vol.6, no. 1 The Mathematical Association

Three Articles on Formative Assessment in Mathematics by Dylan Wiliam

Formative Assessment in Mathematics

Part 1: Rich questioning

Dylan Wiliam

Introduction

Successive governments have bemoaned the 'long tail of underachievement' in British schools, and the clear implication of such a phrase is that achievement in Britain is skewed towards the lower end. In fact, the distribution of achievement in British schools is almost completely symmetrical, and what skew there is is towards the higher end (would we call that a long tail of over-achievement?). While there is no evidence of a skewed distribution, however, it is true that the range of achievement in Britain is wider than in almost any other developed country. Our highest-performing students compare well to the best in any other country, but we have many students who leave school or college without adequate capability in mathematics.

Now the typical argument made by politicians is that this is unacceptable because the lack of an adequately skilled workforce harms our industrial competitiveness, but this argument simply doesn't hold up, because, as many studies have shown, there is no discernable association between levels of academic achievement and industrial productivity.

Nevertheless, I believe we should be concerned about the levels of mathematical achievement of school leavers in this country. The reason for this is that in my view too many of our young people leave school without the mathematical capabilities they need in order to exercise an acceptable degree of control over their own lives.

About a year ago, Paul Black and I published a review of approximately 250 studies, carried out over the last ten years, into the effectiveness of formative assessment in raising standards of achievement [1]. What we found was that increasing the use of formative assessment in school classrooms does produce significant increases in students' learning — enough to raise levels of performance in mathematics amongst British students to fifth place in the international 'league tables' of mathematical performance, behind only Japan, Singapore, Taiwan and South Korea. Put another way, appropriate use of formative assessment would raise the average achievement students by as much as 2 grades at GCSE.

But much more importantly, formative assessment has the power to change the distribution of attainment. Good formative assessment appears to be disproportionately beneficial for lower attainers, so that typically, an average improvement of two GCSE grades would actually be an improvement of three grades for the weakest students, versus an improvement of one grade for the strongest. Formative assessment therefore seems to be the most promising way to reduce the unacceptably wide variation in attainment that currently exist in mathematics classrooms in Britain.

Parts 2 and 3 of this article will appear in future issues of *Equals* and will deal with giving feedback to learners, the importance of sharing learning goals with students, and student self-assessment. The main focus of this first part is with the use of questions to support learning.

What makes a good question?

Two items used in the *Third International Mathematics and Science Study* (TIMSS) are shown in figure 1 below. Although apparently quite similar, the success rates on the two items were very different. For example, in Israel, 88% of the students answered the first items correctly, while only 46% answered the second correctly, with 39% choosing response (b). The reason for this is that many students, in learning about fractions, develop the naive conception that the largest fraction is the one with the smallest denominator, and the smallest fraction is the one with the largest denominator. This approach leads to the correct answer for the first item, but leads to an incorrect response to the second. In this sense, the first item is a much weaker item than the second, because many students can get it right for the wrong reasons.

Item 1 (success rate 88%)

Which fraction is the smallest?

a) $\frac{1}{6}$ b) $\frac{2}{3}$ c) $\frac{1}{3}$ d) $\frac{1}{2}$

Item 2 (success rate 46%)

Which fraction is the largest?

a) $\dfrac{4}{5}$ b) $\dfrac{3}{4}$ c) $\dfrac{5}{8}$ d) $\dfrac{7}{10}$

Figure 1: two items from the Third International Mathematics and Science Study

This illustrates a very general principle in teachers' classroom questioning. By asking questions of students, teachers try to establish whether students have understood what they are meant to be learning, and if students answer the questions correctly, it is tempting to assume that the students' conceptions match those of the teacher. However, all that has really been established is that the students' conceptions fit, within the limitations of the questions. Unless the questions used are very rich, there will be a number of students who manage to give all the right responses, while having very different conceptions from those intended.

A particularly stark example of this is the following pair of simultaneous equations:

$$3a = 24$$
$$a + b = 16$$

Many students find this difficult, often saying that it can't be done. The teacher might conclude that they need some more help with equations of this sort, but the most likely reason for the difficulties with this item is not to with mathematical skills but with their beliefs. If the students are encouraged to talk about their difficulty, they often say things like, "I keep on getting b is 8, but it can't be because a is". The reason that many students have developed such a belief is, of course, that before they were introduced to solving equations, they were almost certainly practising substitution of numbers into algebraic formulas, where each letter stood for a different number. Although the students will not have been taught that each letter must stand for a different number, they have generalised implicit rules from their previous experience (just as because we always show them triangles where the lowest side is horizontal, they talk of "upside-down triangles").

The important point here is that we would not have known about these unintended conceptions if the second equation had been a + b = 17 instead of a + b = 16. Items that reveal unintended conceptions — in other words that provide a "window into thinking" — are difficult to generate, but they are crucially important if we are to improve the quality of students mathematical learning.

Now some people have argued that these unintended conceptions are the result of poor teaching. If only the teacher had phrased their explanation more carefully, had ensured that no unintended features were learnt alongside the intended features, then these misconceptions would not arise.

But this argument fails to acknowledge two important points. The first is that this kind of over-generalisation is a fundamental feature of human thinking. When young children say things like "I goed to the shop yesterday", they are demonstrating a remarkable feat of generalisation. From the huge messiness of the language that they hear around them, they have learnt that to create the past tense of a verb, one adds "ed". In the same way, if one asks young children what causes the wind, the most common answer is "trees". They have not been taught this, but have observed that trees are swaying when the wind is blowing and (like many politicians) have inferred a causation from a correlation.

The second point is that even if we wanted to, we are unable to control the student's environment to the extent necessary for unintended conceptions not to arise. For example, it is well known that many students believe that the result of multiplying 2.3 by 10 is 2.30. It is highly unlikely that they have been taught this. Rather this belief arises as a result of observing regularities in what they see around them. The result of multiplying whole-numbers by 10 is just to put a zero at the end, so why shouldn't that work for all numbers? The only way to prevent students from acquiring this 'misconception' would be to introduce decimals before one introduces multiplying single-digit numbers by 10, which is clearly absurd. The important point is that we must acknowledge that what students learn is not necessarily what the teacher intended, and it is essential that teachers explore students' thinking before assuming that students have 'understood' something.

Now questions that give us this "window into thinking" are hard to find, but within any school there will be a good selection of rich questions in use — the trouble is that each teacher will have her or his stock of good questions, but these questions don't get shared within the school, and are certainly not seen as central to good teaching.

In Britain, most teachers spend most of their lesson preparation time in marking books, invariably doing so alone. In some other countries, the majority of lesson preparation time is spent planning how new topics can be introduced, which contexts and examples will be used, and so on. This is sometimes done individually or with groups of teachers working together. In Japan, however, teachers spend a substantial proportion of their lesson preparation time working together to devise questions to use in order to find out whether their teaching has been successful.

Now, in thinking up good questions, it is important not to allow the traditional concerns of reliability and validity to determine what makes a good question. For example, many teachers think that the following question, taken from the *Chelsea Diagnostic Test for Algebra*, is 'unfair':

Simplify (if possible): 2a + 3b

This item is felt to be unfair because students 'know' that in answering test questions, you have to do some work, so it must be possible to simplify this expression, otherwise the teacher wouldn't have asked the question. And I would agree that to use this item in a test or an examination where the goal is to determine a student's achievement would probably not be a good idea. But to find out whether students understand algebra, it is a very good item indeed. If in the context of classroom work, rather than a formal test or exam, a student can be tempted to 'simplify' 2a + 3b then I want to know that, because it means that I haven't managed to develop in the student a real sense of what algebra is about.

Similar issues are raised by asking students which of these two fractions is the larger:

$$\frac{3}{7} \qquad \frac{3}{11}$$

Now in some senses this is a 'trick question'. There is no doubt that this is a very hard item, with typically only around one 14-year old in six able to give the correct answer (compared with around three-quarters of 14-year-olds being able to select correctly the larger of two 'ordinary' fractions). It may not, therefore, be a very good item to used in a test of students' achievement. But as a teacher, I think it is very important for me to know if my students think that $\frac{3}{11}$ is larger than $\frac{3}{7}$. The fact that this item is seen as a 'trick question' shows how deeply ingrained into our practice the summative function of assessment is.

A third example, that caused considerable disquic amongst teachers when it was used in a national test, based on the following item, again taken from one of th *Chelsea Diagnostic Tests*:

Which of the following statements is true:

(1)   AB is longer than CD

(2)   AB is shorter than CD

(3)   AB and CD are the same length

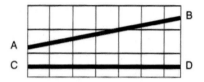

Again, viewed in terms of formal tests and examinations this may be an unfair item, but in terms of a teacher's need to establish secure foundations for future learning, I would argue that this is entirely appropriate.

Rich questioning, of the kind described above, provides teachers not just with evidence about what their students can do, but also what the teacher needs to do next, in order to broaden or deepen understanding.

Classroom questioning

There is also a substantial body of evidence about the most effective ways to use classroom questions. In many schools in this country, teachers tend to use questions as a way of directing the attention of the class, and keeping students 'on task', by scattering questions all around the classroom. This probably does keep the majority of students 'on their toes' but makes only a limited contribution to supporting learning. What is far less frequent in this country is to see a teacher, in a whole-class lesson, have an extended exchange with a single student, involving a second, third, fourth or even fifth follow-up question to the student's initial answer, but with such questions, the level of classroom dialogue can be built up to quite a sophisticated level, with consequent positive effects on learning. Of course, changing one's questioning style is very difficult where students are used to a particular set of practices (and may even regard asking supplementary questions as 'unfair'). And it may even be that other students see extended exchanges between the teacher and another student as a chance to relax and go 'off task', but as soon as students understand that the teacher may well be asking them what they have learned from a particular exchange between another student and the teacher, their concentration is likely to be quite high!

How much time a teacher allows a student to respond before evaluating the response is also important. It is well known that teachers do not allow students much time to answer questions, and, if they don't receive a response quickly, they will 'help' the student by providing a clue or weakening the question in some way, or even moving on to another student. However, what is not widely appreciated is that the amount of time between the student providing an answer and the teacher's evaluation of that answer is much more important. Of course, where the question is a simple matter of factual recall, then allowing a student time to reflect and expand upon the answer is unlikely to help much. But where the question requires thought, then increasing the time between the end of the student's answer and the teacher's evaluation from the average 'wait-time' of less than a second to three seconds, produces measurable increases in learning (although increases beyond three seconds have little effect, and may cause lessons to lose pace).

In fact, questions need not always come from the teacher. There is substantial evidence that students' learning is enhanced by getting them to generate their own questions. If instead of writing an end-of-topic test herself, the teacher asks the students to write a test that tests the work the class has been doing, the teacher can gather useful evidence about what the students think they have been learning, which is often very different from what the teacher thinks the class has been learning. This can be a particularly effective strategy with disaffected older students, who often feel threatened by tests. Asking them to write a test for the topic they have completed, and making clear that the teacher is going to mark the question rather than the answers, can be a hugely liberating experience for many students.

Some researchers have gone even further, and shown that questions can limit classroom discourse, since they tend to demand a simple answer. There is a substantial body of evidence that classroom learning is enhanced considerably by shifting from asking questions to making statements. For example, instead of asking "Are all squares rectangles", which seems to require a 'simple' yes/no answer, the level of classroom discourse (and student learning) is improved considerably by framing the same question as a statement — "All squares are rectangles", and asking students to discuss this in small groups before presenting a reasoned conclusion to the class.

Conclusion

Over thirty years ago, David Ausubel argued that the most important factor influencing learning is what the learner already knows, and that the job of the teacher was to ascertain this and to teach accordingly. Since then it has become abundantly clear that students' naive conceptions are not random aberrations, but the result of sophisticated and creative attempts by students to make sense of their experience. Within a normal mathematics classroom, there is clearly not enough time for the teacher to treat each student as an individual, but the good news is that the vast majority of the naive conceptions are quite commonly shared, and as long as the teacher has a small battery of good questions it will be possible to elicit the most significant of these misconceptions. If the teacher does then have any time to spend with individual students, this can be targeted at those whose misconceptions are not commonly shared. After all, teaching is interesting because students are so different, but it is only possible because they are so similar.

References

1 Black, P. J. & Wiliam, D. (1998). Assessment and classroom learning. *Assessment in Education: Principles Policy and Practice*, 5(1), 7-73.

2 Hart, K. M.; Brown, M. L.; Kerslake, D.; Küchemann, D. & Ruddock, G. (1985). *Chelsea diagnostic mathematics tests.* Windsor, UK: NFER-Nelson.

Dylan Wiliam works at King's College London School of Education. If you have any questions relating to formative assessment that you would like to see discussed in future issues of Equals, please email him at dylan.wiliam@kcl.ac.uk.

Significant Figures

The Cerne Abbas giant is carved in the chalk of the hill above the Sherborne road. The chalk lines are 2 feet wide and are seen for miles. His height is half that of the dome of St.Pauls. He equals 30 tall men standing one on the other; each of his fingers measures 7 feet, and the club in his hand is 40 yards.

Arthur Mee, Dorset, London:
Hodder and Stoughton, 2nd edition, 1967.

Formative Assessment in Mathematics
Part 2: Feedback

Introduction

This is the second of three articles reviewing the effectiveness of formative assessment, summarising the findings of a review of over 200 studies into formative assessment (Black and Wiliam, 1998). The focus of this article is the effect that feedback to learners about their past performance has on their future performance and their attitudes towards their learning. In particular, what kinds of feedback are the most effective in promoting learning?

The quality of feedback

Ruth Butler (1998) investigated the effectiveness of different kinds of feedback on 132 year 7 students in 12 classes in 4 Israeli schools. For the first lesson, the students in each class were given a booklet containing a range of divergent thinking tasks. At the end of the lesson, their work was collected in. This work was then marked by independent markers. At the beginning of the next lesson, two days later, the students were given feedback on the work they had done in the first lesson. In four of the classes students were given marks (which were scaled so as to range from 40 to 99) while in another four of the classes, students were given comments, such as "You thought of quite a few interesting ideas; maybe you could think of more ideas". In the other four classes, the students were given both marks and comments.

Then, the students were asked to attempt some similar tasks, and told that they would get the same sort of feedback as they had received for the first lesson's work. Again, the work was collected in and marked.

Those given only marks made no gain from the first lesson to the second. Those who had received high marks in the tests were interested in the work, but those who had received low marks were not. The students given only comments scored, on average, 30% more on the work done in the second lesson than on the first, and the interest of all the students in the work was high. However, those given both marks and comments made no gain from the first lesson to the second, and those who had received high marks showed high interest while those who received low marks did not.

In other words, far from producing the best effects of both kinds of feedback, giving marks alongside the comments completely washed out the beneficial effects of the comments. The use of both marks and comments is probably the most widespread form of feedback used in the United Kingdom, and yet this study (and others like it–see below) show that it is no more effective than marks alone. In other words, if you are going to grade or mark a piece of work, you are wasting your time writing careful diagnostic comments.

A clear indication of the role that ego plays in learning is given by another study by Ruth Butler (1987). In this study, 200 year 6 and 7 students spent a lesson working on a variety of divergent thinking tasks. Again, the work was collected in and the students were given one of four kinds of feedback on this work at the beginning of the second lesson (again two days later):

a quarter of the students were given comments;

a quarter were given grades;

a quarter were given praise; and

a quarter were given no feedback at all.

The quality of the work done in the second lesson was compared to that done in the first. The quality of work of those given comments had improved substantially compared to the first lesson, but those given grades and praise had made no more progress than those given absolutely no feedback throughout their learning of this topic.

At the end of the second lesson, the students were given a questionnaire about what factors influenced their work. In particular the questionnaire sought to establish whether the students attributed successes and failures to themselves (called ego-involvement) or to the work they were doing (task-involvement). Examples of ego- and task-involving attributions are shown in table 1. (See below.)

Those students given comments during their work on the topic had high levels of task-involvement, but their levels of ego-involvement were the same as those given no feedback. However, those given praise and those

Attribution of	Ego	Task
Effort	To do better than others	Interest
	To avoid doing worse than others	To improve performance
Success	Ability	Interest
	Performance of others	Effort
		Experience of previous learning

Table 1: ego- and task-related attributions

given grades had comparable levels of task-involvement to the control group, but their levels of ego-involvement were substantially higher. The only effect of the grades and the praise, therefore, was to increase the sense of ego-involvement without increasing achievement.

This should not surprise us. In pastoral work, we have known for many years that one should criticize the behaviour, not the child, thus focusing on task-involving rather than ego-involving feedback. These findings are also consistent with the research on praise carried out in the 1970s which showed clearly that praise was not necessarily 'a good thing'-in fact the best teachers appear to praise slightly less than average (Good and Grouws, 1975). It is the quality, rather than the quantity of praise that is important and in particular, teacher praise is far more effective if it is infrequent, credible, contingent, specific, and genuine (Brophy, 1981). It is also essential that praise is related to factors within an individual's control, so that praising a gifted student just for being gifted is likely to lead to negative consequences in the long term.

The timing of feedback is also crucial. If it is given too early, before students have had a chance to work on a problem, then they will learn less. Most of this research has been done in the United States, where it goes under the name of 'peekability research', because the important question is whether students are able to 'peek' at the answers before they have tried to answer the question. However, a British study, undertaken by Simmonds and Cope (1993) found similar results. Pairs of students aged between 9 and 11 worked on angle and rotation problems. Some of these worked on the problems using Logo and some worked on the problems using pencil and paper. The students working in Logo were able to use a 'trial and improvement' strategy which enabled them to get a solution with little

mental effort. However, for those working with pencil and paper, working out the effect of a single rotation was much more time consuming, and thus the students had an incentive to think carefully, and this greater 'mindfulness' led to more learning.

The effects of feedback highlighted above might suggest that the more feedback, the better, but this is not necessarily the case. Day and Cordon (1993) looked at the learning of a group of 64 year 4 students on reasoning tasks. Half of the students were given a 'scaffolded' response when they got stuck — in other words they were given only as much help as they needed to make progress, while the other half were given a complete solution as soon as they got stuck, and then given a new problem to work on. Those given the 'scaffolded' response learnt more, and retained their learning longer than those given full solutions.

In a sense, this is hardly surprising, since those given the complete solutions had the opportunity for learning taken away from them. As well as saving time, therefore, developing skills of 'minimal intervention' promote better learning.

Sometimes, the help need not even be related to the subject matter. Often, when a student is given a new task, the student asks for help immediately. When the teacher asks, "What can't you do?" it is common to hear the reply, "I can't do any of it". In such circumstances, the student's reaction may be caused by anxiety about the unfamiliar nature of the task, and it is frequently possible to support the student by saying something like "Copy out that table, and I'll be back in five minutes to help you fill it in". This is often all the support the student needs. Copying out the table forces the student to look in detail at how the table is laid out, and this 'busy work' can provide time for the student to make sense of the task herself.

The consistency of these messages from research on the effects of feedback extends well beyond school and other educational settings. A review of 131 well-designed studies in educational and workplace settings found that, on average, feedback did improve performance, but this average effect disguised substantial differences between studies. Perhaps most surpisingly, in 40% of the studies, giving feedback had a negative impact on performance. In other words, in two out of every five studies, giving people feedback on their performance made their performance worse than if they were given no feedback on their performance at all! On further investigation, the researchers found that feedback makes performance worse when it is focused on the self-esteem or self-image (as is the case with grades and praise). The use of praise can increase motivation, but then it becomes necessary to use praise all the time to maintain the motivation. In this situation, it is very difficult to maintain praise as genuine and sincere. In contrast, the use of feedback improves performance when it is focused on what needs to be done to improve, and particularly when it gives specific details about how to improve.

This suggests that feedback is not the same as formative assessment. Feedback is a necessary first step, but feedback is formative only if the information fed back to the learner is used by the learner in improving performance. If the information fed back to the learner is intended to be helpful, but cannot be used by the learner in improving her own peformance it is not formative. It is rather like telling an unsuccessful comedian to "be funnier".

As noted above, the quality of feedback is a powerful influence on the way that learners attribute their successes and failures. A series of research studies, carried out by Carol Dweck over twenty years, has shown that different students differ in whether they regard their success and failures as:

being due to 'internal' factors (such as one's own performance) or 'external' factors (such as getting a lenient or a severe marker);

being due to 'stable' factors (such as one's ability) or 'unstable' factors (such as effort or luck); and

applying globally to everything one undertakes, or related only to the specific activity on which one succeeded or failed.

Table 2 gives some examples of attributions of success and failure.(See below.)

Dweck and others have found that boys are more likely to attribute their successes to stable causes (such as ability), and their failures to unstable causes (such as lack of effort and bad luck). This would certainly explain the high degree of confidence with which boys approach examinations for which they are completely unprepared. More controversially, the same research

Attribution of	Success	Failure
locus	internal: "I got a good mark because it was a good piece of work" external: "I got a good mark because the teacher likes me"	internal: "I got a low mark because it wasn't a very good piece of work" external: "I got a low mark because the teacher doesn't like me
stability	stable: "I got a good exam-mark because I'm good at that subject" unstable: "I got a good exam-mark because I was lucky in the questions that came up"	stable: I got a bad exam-mark because I'm no good at that subject" unstable: "I got a bad exam-mark because hadn't done any revision"
specificity	specific: "I'm good at that but that's the only thing I'm good at" global: "I'm good at that means I'll be good at everything"	specific: "I'm no good at that but I'm good at everything else" global: "I'm useless at everything"

Table 2: dimensions of attributions of success and failure

suggests that girls attribute their successes to unstable causes (such as effort) and their failures to stable causes (such as lack of ability), leading to what has been termed 'learned helplessness'.

More recent work in this area suggests that what matters more, in terms of motivation, is whether students see ability as fixed or incremental. Students who believe that ability is fixed will see any piece of work that they are given as a chance either to re-affirm their ability, or to be 'shown-up'. If they are confident in their ability to achieve what is asked of them, then they will attempt the task. However, if their confidence in their ability to carry out their task is low, then they will avoid the challenge, and this can be seen in mathematics classrooms up and down the country every day. Taking all things into account, a large number of students decide that they would rather be thought lazy than stupid, and refuse to engage with the task, and this is a direct consequence of the belief that ability is fixed. In contrast, those who see ability as incremental see all challenges as chances to learn-to get cleverer-and therefore in the face of failure will try harder. What is perhaps most important here is that these views of ability are generally not global-the same students often believe that ability in schoolwork is fixed, while at the same time believe that ability in athletics is incremental, in that the more one trains, the more one's ability increases. What we therefore need to do is to ensure that the feedback we give students supports a view of ability as incremental rather than fixed.

Summary
Perhaps surprisingly for educational research, the research on feedback paints a remarkably coherent picture. Feedback to learners should focus on what they need to do to improve, rather than on how well they have done, and should avoid comparison with others. Students who are used to having every piece of work graded will resist this, wanting to know whether a particular piece of work is good or not, and in some cases, depending on the situation, the teacher may need to go along with this. In the long term, however, we should aim to reduce the amount of ego-involving feedback we give to learners (and with new entrants to the school, perhaps not begin the process at all!), and focus on the student's learning needs. Furthermore, feedback should not just tell students to work harder or be 'more systematic'-the feedback should contain a

recipe for future action, otherwise it is not formative. Finally, feedback should be designed so as to lead all students to believe that ability-even in mathematics-is incremental. In other words the more we 'train' at mathematics, the clever we get.

Although there is a clear set of priorities for the development of feedback, there is no 'one right way' to do this. The feedback routines in each class will need to be thoroughly integrated into the daily work of the class, and so it will look slightly different in every classroom. This means that no-one can tell teachers how this should be done-it will be a matter for each teacher to work out a way of incorporating some of these ideas into her or his own practice. However, the size of the effects found in the experiments discussed above, and in the other research reviewed by Black and Wiliam suggests that changing the kinds of feedback we use in mathematics classrooms could have more effect than all the government initiatives put together.

School of Education Kings College. London

References

Black, P. J. & Wiliam, D. (1998). Assessment and classroom learning. Assessment in Education: Principles Policy and Practice, 5(1), 7-73.

Brophy, J. (1981) Teacher praise: a functional analysis. Review of Educational Research 51 (1) 5-32.

Butler, R. (1988) Enhancing and undermining intrinsic motivation; the effects of task-involving and ego-involving evaluation on interest and performance. British Journal of Educational Psychology 58 1-14

Butler, R. (1987) Task-involving and ego-involving properties of evaluation: effects of different feedback conditions on motivational perceptions, interest and performance. Journal of Educational Psychology 79 (4) 474-482.

Dweck, C. S. (1986). Motivational processes affecting learning. American Psychologist, 41(10), 1040-1048.

Good, T. L. and Grouws, D. A. (1975). Process-product relationships in fourth grade mathematics clasrooms. Report for National Institute of Education, Columbia, MO: University of Missouri (report no NE-G-00-0-0123).

Kluger, A. N. & DeNisi, A. (1996). The effects of feedback interventions on performance: a historical review, a meta-analysis, and a preliminary feedback intervention theory. Psychological Bulletin, 119(2), 254-284.

Formative Assessment in Mathematics

Part 3: The Learner's Role

Dylan Wiliam

Introduction

This is the last of three articles reviewing the effectiveness of formative assessment, summarising the findings of a review of over 200 studies into formative assessment (Black and Wiliam, 1998). The first two articles dealt with the teacher's role in questioning and in giving feedback to learners. This last article focuses on the role of the learner in formative assessment, specifically the idea of sharing criteria with learners and student self-assessment. For each of these two ideas, I describe in detail below one experiment that has shown how effective involving students in these ways can be, and then go on to describe how they relate to research that we are currently doing with mathematics and science teachers.

Sharing criteria with learners

Frederiksen and White (1997) undertook a study of three teachers, each of whom taught 4 parallel Y8 classes in two US schools. The average size of the classes was 31. In order to assess the representativeness of the sample, all the students in the study were given a basic skills test, and their scores were close to the national average. All twelve classes followed a novel curriculum (called *Thinker Tools*) for a term. The curriculum had been designed to promote thinking in the science classroom through a focus on a series of seven scientific investigations (approximately two weeks each). Each investigation incorporated a series of evaluation activities. In half of each teacher's classes these evaluation episodes took the form of a discussion about what they liked and disliked about the topic. For the other two classes they engaged in a process of 'reflective assessment'. Through a series of small-group and individual activities, the students were introduced to the nine assessment criteria (each of which was assessed on a 5-point scale) that the teacher would use in evaluating their work. At the end of each episode within an investigation, the students were asked to assess their performance against two of the criteria, and at the end of the investigation, students had to assess their performance against all nine. Whenever they assessed themselves, they had to write a brief statement showing which aspects of their work formed the basis for their rating. At the end of each investigation, students presented their work to the class, and the students used the criteria to give each other feedback.

As well as the students' self-evaluations, the teachers also assessed each investigation, scoring both the quality of the presentation and the quality of the written report, each being scored on a 1 to 5 scale. The possible score on each of the seven investigations therefore ranged from 2 to 10.

The mean project scores achieved by the students in

the two groups over the seven investigations are summarised in Table 1, classified according to their score on the basic skills test.

Score on basic skills test

Group	Low	Intermediate	High
Likes and dislikes	4.6	5.9	6.6
Reflective assessment	6.7	7.2	7.4

Table 1: Mean project scores for students

Note: the 95% confidence interval for each of these means is approximately 0.5 either side of the mean

Two features are immediately apparent in these data. The first is that the mean scores are higher for the students doing 'reflective assessment', when compared with the control group-in other words, all students improved their scores when they thought about what it was that was to count as good work. However, much more significantly, the difference between the 'likes and dislikes' group and the 'assessment' group was much greater for students with weak basic skills. This suggests that, at least in part, low achievement in schools is exacerbated by students' not understanding what it is they are meant to be doing-an interpretation borne out by the work of Eddie Gray and David Tall (1994), who have shown that 'low-attainers' often struggle because what they are trying to do is actually much harder than what the 'high-attainers' are doing. This study, and others like it, shows how important it is to ensure that students understand the criteria against which their work will be assessed. Otherwise we are in danger of producing students who do not understand what is important and what is not. As the old joke about project work has it: "four weeks on the cover and two on the contents".

Now although it is clear that students need to understand the standards against which their work will be assessed, the study by Frederisken and White shows that the criteria themselves are only the starting point. At the beginning, the words do not have the meaning for the student that they have for the teacher. Just giving 'quality criteria' or 'success criteria' to students will not work, unless students have a chance to see what this might mean in the context of their own work.

Because we understand the meanings of the criteria that we work with, it is tempting to think of them as

definitions of quality, but in truth, they are more like labels we use to talk about ideas in our heads. For example, 'being systematic' in an investigation is not something we can define explicitly, but we can help students develop what Guy Claxton calls a 'nose for quality'.

One of the easiest ways of doing this is to do what Frederiksen and White did. Marking schemes are shared with students, but they are given time to think through, in discussion with others, what this might mean in practice, applied to their own work. We shouldn't assume that the students will understand these right away, but the criteria will provide a focus for negotiating with students about what counts as quality in the mathematics classroom

Another way of helping students understand the criteria for success is, before asking the students to embark on (say) an investigation, to get them to look at the work of other students (suitably anonymised) on similar (although not, of course the same) investigations. In small groups, they can then be asked to decide which of pieces of students' work are good investigations, and why. It is not necessary, or even desirable, for the students to come to firm conclusions and a definition of quality-what is crucial is that they have an opportunity to explore notions of 'quality' for themselves. Spending time looking at other students' work, rather than producing their own work, may seem like 'time off-task', but the evidence is that it is a considerable benefit, particularly for 'low-attainers'.

Student self-assessment

Whether students can really assess their own performance objectively is a matter of heated debate, but very often the debate takes place at cross-purposes. Opponents of self-assessment say that students cannot possibly assess their own performance objectively, but this is an argument about summative self-assessment, and no-one is seriously suggesting that students ought to be able to write their own GCSE certificates! Advocates of self-assessment point out that accuracy is a secondary concern-what really matters is whether self-assessment can enhance learning.

The power of student self-assessment is shown very clearly in an experiment by Fontana and Fernandez (1994). A group of 25 Portuguese primary school teachers met for two hours each week over a twenty-week period during which they were trained in the use of a structured approach to student self-assessment. The approach to self-assessment involved an exploratory component and a prescriptive component. In the exploratory component, each day, at a set time, students organised and carried out individual plans of work, choosing tasks from a range offered to them by the teacher, and had to evaluate their performance against their plans once each week. The progression within the exploratory component had two strands-over the twenty weeks, the tasks and areas in which the students worked were to take on the student's own ideas more and more, and secondly, the criteria that the students used to assess themselves were to become more objective and precise.

The prescriptive component took the form of a series of activities, organised hierarchically, with the choice of activity made by the teacher on the basis of diagnostic assessments of the students. During the first two weeks, children chose from a set of carefully structured tasks, and were then asked to assess themselves. For the next four weeks, students constructed their own mathematical problems following the patterns of those used in weeks 1 and 2, and evaluated them as before, but were required to identify any problems they had, and whether they had sought appropriate help from the teacher.

Over the next four weeks, students were given further sets of learning objectives by the teacher, and again had to devise problems, but now, they were not given examples by the teacher. Finally, in the last ten weeks, students were allowed to set their own learning objectives, to construct relevant mathematical problems, to select appropriate apparatus, and to identify suitable self-assesssments.

Another 20 teachers, matched in terms of age, qualifications, experience, using the same curriculum scheme, for the same amount of time, and doing the same amount of inservice training, acted as a control group. The 354 students being taught by the 25 teachers using self-assessment, and the 313 students being taught by the 20 teachers acting as a control group were each given the same mathematics test at the beginning of the project, and again at the end of the project. Over the course of the experiment, the marks of the students taught by the control-group teachers improved by 7.8 marks. The marks of the students taught by the teachers developing self-assessment improved by 15 marks-

almost twice as big an improvment.

Now the details of the particular approach to self-assessment are not given in the paper, and are in any case not that important-Portuguese primary schools are, after all, very different from British ones. However this is just one of a huge range of studies, in different countries, and looking at students of different ages, that have found a similar pattern. Involving students in assessing their own learning improves that learning.

Putting formative assessment into practice
At the moment we are working with 24 teachers (12 science teachers and 12 mathematics teachers) in six schools to see how the ideas about effective formative assessment we have synthesized from the research literature can be incorporated into day-to-day classroom practice. As well as improving questioning, comment-only marking and the use of students' work to exemplify quality, the teachers are trying out a number of strategies related to student self-assessment.

For example, half the teachers are using 'traffic-lights' or 'smiley faces' to develop students' self-assessment skills. The teacher identifies a number of objectives for the lesson, which are made as clear as possible to the students at the beginning of the lesson. At the end of the lesson, students are asked to indicate their understanding of each objective by a coloured blob or a face. This provides useful feedback to the teacher at two levels. She can see if there are any parts of the lesson that it would be worth re-doing with the whole class, but also she will get feedback about which students would particularly benefit from individual support. However, the real benefit of such a system is that it forces the student to reflect on what she or he has been learning.

Level of understanding	traffic light	smiley face
good understanding	green	☺
not sure	yellow (amber)	😐
don't understand at all	red	☹

This feature of 'mindfulness' is one of the crucial features of effective formative assessment-effective learning involves having most of the students thinking most of the time. Effective questioning is that which

85

engages all students in thinking, rather than remembering, and doesn't allow students to relax simply because they've just answered a question, which means that it can't be their turn again until everyone else has been asked a question.

This notion of 'mindfulness' also gives some clues about what sort of marking is most helpful. Many teachers say that formative feedback is less useful in mathematics, because an answer is either wrong or right. But even where answers are wrong or right, we can still encourage students to think. For example, rather than marking answers right and wrong and telling the students to do corrections, teachers could, instead, feed back saying simply "Three of these ten questions are wrong. Find out which ones and correct them". After all, we are often telling our students to check their work, but rarely help them develop the skills to do so.

Other teachers are experimenting with 'end-of-lesson' reviews. The idea here is that at the beginning of the lesson, one student is appointed as a 'rapporteur' for the lesson. The teacher then teaches a whole-class lesson on some topic, and finishes the lesson ten or fifteen minutes before the end of the lesson. The student rapporteur then gives a summary of the main points of the lesson, and tries to answer any remaining questions that students in the class may have. If he or she can't answer the questions, then the rapporteur asks members of the class to help out. What is surprising is that teachers who have tried this out have found that students are queuing up to play the role of rapporteur, provided this is started at the beginning of the school year, or even better, when students are new to the school (year 1, year 3 or year 7).

Summary
Although at first sight quite different, the four elements of effective formative assessment outlined in this and the previous two papers form a coherent set of strategies for raising achievement, particularly for low-attainers. Rich questioning and effective feedback focus on the teacher's role-first being clear about where we want students to get to, asking appropriate questions to find out where they are, and feeding back to students in ways that the students can use in improving their own performance. Sharing criteria with learners and student self-assessment focus on the learners role-first being clear about where they want to get to, and then monitoring their own progress towards that goal.

To be effective, these strategies must be embedded into the day-to-day life of the classroom, and must be integrated into whatever curriculum scheme is being used. That is why there can be no recipe that will work for everyone. Each teacher will have to find a way of incorporating these ideas into their own practice, and effective formative assessment will look very different in different classrooms. It will, however, have some distinguishing features. Students will be thinking more often than they are trying to remember something, they will believe that by working hard, they get cleverer, they will understand what they are working towards, and will know how they are progressing.

In some ways, this is an old-fashioned message-very similar to the 'good practice' guidelines that were published by HMI in the 1970s and 1980s. What is new is that we now have hard empirical evidence that quality learning does lead to higher achievement. Teachers do not have to choose between teaching well on the one hand and getting good results on the other. Even if all a school cares about is improving its national test scores and exam results, the evidence is that working on formative assessment is the best way to do it. The bonus is that it also leads to better quality learning.

Kings College, London

References

Black, P. J. & Wiliam, D. (1998). Assessment and classroom learning. Assessment in Education: Principles Policy and Practice, 5(1), 7-73.

Fontana, D. & Fernandes, M. (1994). Improvements in mathematics performance as a consequence of self-assessment in Portugese primary school pupils. British Journal of Educational Psychology, 64, 407-417.

Frederiksen, J. R. & White, B. Y. (1997). Reflective assessment of students' research within an inquiry-based middle school science curriculum. Paper presented at the Annual meeting of the American Educational Research Association. Chicago, IL.

Gray, E. M. & Tall, D. O. (1994). Duality, ambiguity and flexibility: a 'proceptual' view of simple arithmetic. Journal for Research in Mathematics Education, 25(2), 116-140.

86